Civil Economy

Civil Economy

Another Idea of the Market

Luigino Bruni
and
Stefano Zamagni

agenda

English translation © Agenda Publishing Ltd 2016
Translated by N. Michael Brennen

First published as *L'Economia Civile*, © Società editrice il Mulino 2015

First English-language edition published in 2016 by Agenda
Agenda Publishing Limited
The Core
Science Central
Bath Lane
Newcastle upon Tyne
NE4 5TF
www.agendapub.com

ISBN 978-1-911116-01-1 (hardcover)
ISBN 978-1-911116-00-4 (paperback)

British Library Cataloguing-in-Publication Data
A catalogue record for this book is available from the British Library

Typeset by JS Typesetting Ltd, Porthcawl, Mid Glamorgan
Printed and bound in the UK by CPI Group (UK) Ltd, Croydon, CR0 4YY

Contents

Preface

We make light of virtues in life; we praise them in death.
  – Giacomo Leopardi, *Nelle nozze della Sorella Paolina*,
                                                    Canti IV, 1824

The world suffers for lack of thought.
  – Pope Paul VI, Encyclical on the Development of Peoples,
                                                    26 March 1967

We have worked in the area of the civil economy for many years. We published a large work on this theme in 2007, which was a time of growth and enthusiasm for the new financial economy that promised widespread and inclusive well-being. Actually, even then we were pointing out the serious limits of a vision of the market and a conception of the company that was based on the individual rather than on the person, on compulsively seeking wealth rather than public happiness, and forgetting and destroying such fundamental economic goods as relational goods, common goods, and gratuitous goods. The crisis that exploded in 2007–8 only reinforced our diagnosis of the malady of a particular capitalist economic system that is wholly centred on rent seeking.[1] The crisis confirmed yet again that the classic tradition of the civil economy still has a future for Europe and for everyone.

As well as witnessing the grave crisis of debt-based financial capitalism (private debt in the United States and public debt in Europe) the past ten years have been an important time for the civil economy. An unintended consequence of the crisis was to create cultural conditions suitable for understanding the economic, social and ethical relevance of a different, sustainable vision of the economy and finance. The "civil economy" is a tradition of thought that, in order to save the market economy, recalls it to its ancient, original vocation as an ally of the common good, representing a space for liberty, sociality and the expression of our capabilities and "vocations" as persons, particularly the vocation of work.

We will not exit this serious crisis, which goes much deeper than just the economic dimension, by eliminating finance and markets (assuming that someone were even able to do so), but only with civil and civilizing finance and markets. Indeed, we should recall one of the lessons of the civil economy tradition: actual markets, different from those described in most textbooks, are never ethically neutral; they are either civil or uncivil (*tertium non datur*, i.e. "no middle ground"). If finance and markets do not create value and *values*, if they do not create work, if they do not respect and care for the environment, they are simply uncivil; they destroy the economy and civilizations, as we continue to see in this time of crisis. The market economy will survive only if it is able to move beyond this form of individualistic, financial capitalism, towards a civil and civilizing economy.

---

1. "Rent-seeking" is not related to renting space in which to live or work. It is a technical expression in contemporary economics that describes the socially costly pursuit of wealth transfers. The idea is a cornerstone of public choice theory, and the goal is to profit by extracting money, or benefits from others through transfers rather than through market exchanges.

It is useful to recall at this point that the civil economy has two main meanings. The "Civil Economy", written with initial capitals, is a tradition of thought and a perspective for studying the economy that understands the *entire* economy differently from the dominant Anglo-American capitalist tradition. This first meaning is not directly related to the third sector,[2] much less the non-profit sector (a concept and expression originating, not by chance, in the United States, which does not understand the specific nature of the Civil Economy). The Civil Economy speaks to the whole of the economy and to society, offering a standard of judgement for choices and action by governments, multinationals, consumers (ethical consumption) and socially responsible savers.

There is also the "civil economy", not capitalized, that can be synonymous – without completely overlapping them – with expressions such as social economy, private-social organizations, value-based organizations, solidarity economy, popular economy and so forth. This second meaning of the civil economy has its own specific characteristics and originality, as it includes actors who remain outside other conceptions and definitions. Among these are traditional forms of co-operation – such as credit, production, use and consumption – as well as new projects like the Economy of Communion, which due to their legal forms or traditions are not part of the non-profit sector, nor of certain more anti-market definitions of social economy.[3]

The crisis years have seen the growth of the civil economy in both senses. Indeed, on the one hand, academic interest from an increasingly international group of scholars has grown (of which the

---

2. The term "third sector", as opposed to the public and private sectors, refers to non-profit organizations, including voluntary groups, foundations, social cooperatives, social enterprises and NGOs.

3. For stylistic reasons the lower-case term has been used throughout the book but it should be understood in the first (capitalized) sense. (*Trans.*)

translation of our 2004 work into six foreign languages is eloquent proof). In addition, a movement has grown that is made up of those who believe in and work for communal and solidarity enterprises, and those who conceive of the market as the practice of civil virtues and ethical and spiritual engagement.

The Civil Economy is basically a paradigm, a map that guides us. It has a sense of causation, and is not just a theory or a specific model. We assign two specific goals to it. The first is to contribute towards filling the cultural void in economic thinking, which has been neglected for far too long. It should be evident to anyone that the current crisis is also the result of the superficial credence with which the broad public and policy makers perceive and receive the prescriptions of the many influential think-tanks scattered around the world. With a high level of technical sophistication in their research techniques, these think-tanks have succeeded in passing off their explanations of how financial markets work as true (and certain) and in having their recommendations accepted as incontrovertible.

The second goal we entrust to the Civil Economy paradigm is to contribute towards counteracting both the serious productivity decline of our production systems over the past twenty years and the insufficient capacity for innovation in our companies. We are of the view that at the bottom of this dismal state of affairs there is, in addition to an inadequate institutional structure, a concept of work that is obsolete in the era of the so-called fourth industrial revolution. That concept still depends excessively on Frederick Taylor's efficiency model,[4] which is not able to attribute value to the

---

4. Frederick Taylor (1856–1915) was an American mechanical engineer who applied the principles of engineering to factory work in order to improve efficiency. His *The Principles of Scientific Management* (1911) became a management best-seller.

principle of co-operation, or to see the market as a place for mutual assistance and work as an opportunity for human flourishing, not just fatigue and boredom.

We offer the invitation with which Antonio Genovesi closed his *Lezioni di economia civile* (*Lessons of Civil Economy*):

> The idea behind this work is this: if we fix our eyes on such a beautiful and useful truth, we will study not out of pedantic vanity, nor out of pride to lord it over the ignorant, nor out of perversity to circumvent them, but instead to comply with the law of the Moderator of the world, who commands us to use our ingenuity to be useful to one another.[5]
>
> (Genovesi 1765–70)

This short volume represents new thinking. It is by now a recognized fact that market systems are compatible with cultures of many different origins and forms. In turn, the degree of compatibility of market systems with cultures has effects on the efficiency and sustainability of the systems themselves. What we say in the following pages does not mean dropping the advances of the analysis made over the last century. It does mean recognizing the urgency of rethinking the anthropological foundation of economic discourse, which continues to embody an excessively narrow conception of personal well-being and that takes little account of human capacities for moral sentiments going beyond the mere accounting of personal gains. It is a fact that when people define their own interests and when they act to pursue those interests, they more often than not give great weight to their moral premises and to the principle of reciprocity.

---

5. Unless otherwise noted, all translations from the Italian originals are by the translator.

One of the most penetrating dangers of our time, coined by the twentieth-century author C. S. Lewis, is "chronological snobbery": the uncritical acceptance of anything merely because it belongs to the intellectual trends of our present. This short book has been written precisely as a contribution to repulse such danger.

Part I

History

1

What is civil economy?

[A]t a severe crisis, when lives in multitudes and wealth in masses are at stake, the political economists are helpless – practically mute: no demonstrable solution of the difficulty can be given by them, such as may convince or calm the opposing parties.

– John Ruskin, *Unto This Last*, 1860

We need to begin anew to criticize the capitalism we have created in the past three decades, a period that coincides with the era of globalization and common goods. The beginning of the 1980s marked the close of an energetic time of reflection on economic and political systems. The late 1970s ended (primarily in Europe) an era of just under three centuries characterized by the Industrial Revolution, and an era characterized by schools of thought critical of this new form of production and life, which has been called "capitalism" since Karl Marx's time. With globalization and the collapse of state socialism, the economy as it manifests itself in present history became a fact of nature, the deep structure of which was no longer discussed. That is not to say that there are no contemporary economists, politicians, or philosophers who criticize our form of capitalism – one need only consider Amartya Sen, Muhammad Yunus or Serge Latouche – but these criticisms as a whole have not yet produced a different narrative of our time. Important innovations have been proposed in both theory and practice, but without either individually or collectively having the strength of thought to narrate a non-capitalist market economy. Sen's capabilities, Yunus's social business, Joseph Stiglitz's and Thomas Piketty's criticisms of inequality, Vandava Shiva's "earth-centred economy" and Latouche's degrowth all differ among themselves, but even if we were able to systematically arrange them in such a way as to make them coherently coexist (not an easy task), we still would not have created an alternative market economy to the current form of capitalism. In truth, we would have to say that we are far from it. We are like the baby in its mother's womb, so immersed in the liquid that nourishes it that it cannot think that a world beyond might exist; to become aware of the existence of another larger, more marvellous world it must first leave the world that nurtures and sustains it.

Although the tone of this opening paragraph might lead some to think that we are about to define the civil economy as the true alternative to this form of capitalism, in reality the civil economy is not that alternate system, neither in thought nor practice. It is, however, a laboratory of thought and practice in which we can attempt to imagine it. It is an inclusive and open process in which there is room for all not content with today's financial capitalism and who, within a few broad cultural coordinates, seek a deeper understanding that can give rise to more radical and penetrating questions against our current system than those currently posed from within it – perhaps from the perspective of a child born today in the Congo, or in Europe twenty years from now. These children have the right to ask challenging questions about our growth model and our lifestyles. Our non-questioning attitude of today is making their lives harder, at times changing them for the worse and at times for the better, but without them having a say in things. As part of her ethical task a scholar, and certainly a researcher in the civil economy, can ask the questions distant and future children might pose. To ask them correctly she must know the contemporary debates, but she must also study history and the classics because there are many questions from the past that we today have set aside, questions that are now even more pressing. Of course, not all of the past is useful today, and neither are all past questions relevant for understanding and improving the present, but there is a living past that constitutes the roots of our present, and if carefully heard and deciphered, it can help us formulate questions that are less short-sighted and less narrowly focused only on today's interests and fashions.

The civil economy can inspire new thought that is capable of deep questions. It presents a different story about the market, an alternative path to a market economy than the one presented by the dominant system that shapes our world and minds today. In this study we will begin with the central questions of the civil economy tradition and use them to look at the present and future world, ourselves, our companies, our market, our relationships, and our way of life. The ancient world has passed; it is no longer capable of offering us grand narratives able to make us dream, to awaken us in the morning with the enthusiasm to recount and build a history. Writing about the civil economy is then an exercise in the common good, an exercise in what Antonio Rosmini, the nineteenth-century Italian priest and philosopher, described as "intellectual charity"; it is the highest form of charity in an age that suffers from a lack of engaged thought, stories and dreams. And when we lack history, stories and dreams (including the foundational dreams of entrepreneurs) our imaginary is filled with things that end up extinguishing our will to live – and with it the will to go into business, which is an expression of the human passion of a well-rounded life.

This book is an introduction to the civil economy, its history and ideas, presenting the thought of a few of its chief protagonists as well as other economists and social scientists whom we consider exemplary proponents, either implicitly or explicitly, of this vision of the economy; they include Antonio Genovesi, Giacinto Dragonetti, Achille Loria, Amintore Fanfani, John Ruskin and Giorgio Fuà. This is but a partial, idiosyncratic and incomplete list of the "classic" people of the civil economy. A more objective and complete list would certainly need to include Antonio Rosmini, Luigi Sturzo, Luigi Einaudi and Giuseppe Toniolo, and in the twentieth century Paolo Sylos Labini, Federico Caffè, François Perroux and Giacomo Becattini, authors who we will cite only occasionally but who are very present in our perspective. Perhaps the list should not contain writers such as Ruskin and Loria, whom we include not only for a certain intellectual affinity, but to indicate that the civil economy should not remain exclusively Italian or Catholic.

The first step in approaching the civil economy is to imagine it as a symphony. It should not be thought of as either a systematic scientific treatise or a fresco to observe and consider as a complete and final work. A symphony, although based on a score written centuries ago, lives anew *while* it is performed, with an essential role for the musicians, conductor, and audience. It is an "experiential good", the value of which emerges only while the experience happens. This is also the case for the civil economy, which lives in the harmony of many notes and instruments both old and new. For it to be understood, it cannot be reduced to a single movement, or to the individual parts for solo violin or piano, though they are there. It is clear then that to say "civil economy" is to say many things at the same time, all coessential, different and alive.

It is a tradition of thought and writings that had its golden age in the Kingdom of Naples in the second half of the eighteenth century, roughly between the time of the philosopher Giambattista Vico

(d. 1744) and the Parthenopean Republic (1799). It was a tradition with roots in the civilization of the medieval towns, its monasteries, its arts and trades, and in the Franciscan and Dominican traditions, as well as roots that went back to the *areté/virtus*, *polis/civitas* and *eudaimonia/felicitas publica* traditions of the Greek and Roman worlds.

This ancient and noble Italian and European tradition suffered an initial rift at the time of the Bourbon Restoration (1814–30), and then again with the Risorgimento, when writers and philosophers saw all that had come before as *ancien régime*, as an expression of feudalism. The rift was not the death of the tradition, but it did sink into the depths of our culture. It re-emerged from time to time, giving life to important economic and social phenomena (such as cooperative movements, industrial districts and the Olivetti experience) and inspiring intellectuals and economists, a few of whom we will befriend later. The authors we place under the broad umbrella of the civil economy differ widely among themselves (liberals, cooperationists, socialists); this is not to force their thought, much less make them a means to an end unbeknownst to them, but to make the civil economy a pluralistic and culturally "biodiversified" space that goes beyond ideological barriers inside and outside academia. No one author, either of yesterday or today, completely exhausts it; no single vision of the world fully expresses it; no one experience dominates it.

The civil economy, then, is an approach to the market and the economy in Europe – particularly the Europe of Latin and communal origins – that is not founded on the cornerstone of the individual and his freedom *from* the community. Differing from the political economy tradition, the civil economy is a relational and social economy, and "catholic" in the etymological sense (as we will see later with Fanfani).

The civil economy, an ancient, living tree – like a centuries-old olive tree – that is still capable of flowering and bearing fruit, also provides a way of critically evaluating our own time to improve it. To this end it impacts upon policy, labour, finance, banks and businesses. Today we lack many things because we lack a grand narrative of our roots and thus of our future. Innovations do not happen without roots and trees – let us not forget that "innovation" is used in botany for new sprouts. Europe, having lost contact with its humanist roots and the civil economy tree, is no longer innovating. Ultimately, the civil economy is a grand narrative on the vocation and destiny of our past, present and future. This vocation and destiny are at the centre of the thoughts and actions of the authors of this book.

Recounting and living a different history

The civil economy is an inclusive, biodiverse process. As we have said, it is not simply another name for the non-profit economy or third sector, as it involves and addresses the *entire* economy, which it judges either civil or uncivil. Rather, for reasons we will partially see, it is set in opposition to the idea that a separation exists between the *for*-profit and the *non*-profit economies, a separation characteristic of the humanism of Protestant-originated political economy. It is a way of seeing the market, primarily its cooperative nature.

Cooperation – or mutual assistance to use Antonio Genovesi's terminology – is indeed a noted and even a dominant characteristic of the civil economy's idea of the market. However, it would be a mistake to think that understanding the market in terms of cooperation is a prerogative of the civil economy alone. We all know – even the (better) economists both past and present – that communities flourish when they are capable of cooperating. Had we never begun to cooperate (i.e. act together) a common life would never have begun, and we would have remained evolutionarily blocked in a pre-human stage. But as often happens with the great words of humanity, cooperation is at once one and many, often ambivalent, and its most relevant forms are those that are less obvious. Every time people act together to achieve a common and mutually advantageous outcome, we are talking about cooperation.

A hospital, a religious liturgy, a school lesson, a company, a government action and abducting someone are all forms of cooperation, but these are all very different from each other. From this we can derive an initial conclusion: not all forms of cooperation are good. Although some increase the advantages of those involved, they diminish the common good, as those outside are harmed. To distinguish between good and bad forms of cooperation it is first of all necessary to look at the effects they intentionally produce on those outside of them.

Over the course of history, political and economic theories divide into two great families: those that start from the hypothesis that human beings are not naturally capable of cooperating, and those that claim that persons are cooperative by nature. The main representative of the latter tradition is Aristotle: humans are political animals, capable of dialogue with others, of friendship or *philia*, and cooperation for the good of the *polis*. The most radical proponent of the unsociable animal is the English philosopher, Thomas Hobbes (1588–1679): "It is true, that certain living creatures, as Bees, and Ants, live sociably one with another ... therefore some man may perhaps desire to know, why Man-kind cannot do the same" (*Leviathan*, II.XVII). A large part of modern political and social philosophy works within this antisocial tradition, while the ancients and medievals (including Thomas Aquinas) were generally of Aristotle's view. We can also say that the principal question of modern political and economic theory has been how cooperative outcomes can emerge from human beings who are not capable of intentional cooperation because they are dominated by selfish or egocentric interests.

Many (not all) social contract theories are the response of modern political philosophy to that question: egoistic, rational individuals understand that it is in their interest to give life to a civil society by means of an artificial social contract. The natural human is uncivil, thus civil society is artificial. The response of modern economic science to that same question is instead represented by the various theories of the "invisible hand", in which the total good ("the wealth of nations") does not happen by the intentional and natural cooperative action of social animals, but by the interplay of the private interests of egoistic individuals separated among themselves. Underlying these two responses we find the same anthropological hypothesis: the human being is "warped wood" that, without needing to be straightened, produces good "cities" if she is capable of giving life to artificial institutions (the social contract and the market) that transform self-interested passions into collective advantage or well-being.

A different market

It is at this point that a mystery of the market reveals itself. When we open a mainstream textbook on economics, we find that no joint action between the "cooperating" individuals is required for market cooperation. When we enter a shop to buy bread, the encounter between the buyer and the seller is neither described nor lived as an act of intentional cooperation: each one seeks his own interest and fulfils the requisite compensation (money for bread, bread for money) only as a means to obtaining a benefit. And yet that exchange improves the condition of both, thanks to a form of cooperation that requires no joint action. The total good then becomes the sum of private interests of reciprocally immune individuals who cooperate without meeting, touching or looking at each other.[1]

According to mainstream economic theory, it is rather *within* the company that we find intentional or strong cooperation, with the company being a network of joint cooperative actions towards goals that are in large part common. So, when I buy a ticket from Rome to Malaga, there is no form of intentional cooperation between me and the airline; there are only separate and parallel interests of flight and profit. Between the crew members of that flight, however, there must be strong, explicit and intentional cooperation. Consequently, while (almost) no economist would write a theory of the market based on a virtue ethic, conversely with the theory of firms and organizations, there are by now many business ethics based on the virtue ethics of Aristotle and Aquinas. The division of labour in markets and the broader society is a large scale involuntary, implicit cooperation; the division of labour within the company is instead cooperation in the strong sense of a voluntary, joint act. The capitalism of Anglo-Saxon and Protestant origins has given rise to a dichotomous economic theory, which is a version of the Lutheran and Augustinian "two kingdoms" doctrine. In markets there is implicit, weak and non-intentional cooperation; in the firm, and generally in organizations, we find instead explicit, strong and

---

1. Here and elsewhere the term *immune* is used in contrast to *commune* or *communal*. A *community* is a group bound together around the *munus*, which has both the sense of gift and duty; a gift as *munus* is one that may be obligatory and which in turn obliges the recipient to respond. One who is *immune* is exempt from the reciprocally obliging and obligatory communal system of *munus*. In contrast to gift as *munus*, the authors propose that we understand gift as *donum*, a gift that does not expect or require a certain response. Such a gift is *gratuitous*, given *gratuitously*, as will be seen in the rest of the work. (*Trans.*).

intentional cooperation: two forms of cooperation, two "cities", profoundly and naturally different from each other.

However, this is not the only possible type of cooperation in markets. The civil economy views the economy and the market differently. Here the distinction between *ad intra* (within the firm) and *ad extra* (in the market) cooperation was never prevalent, at least not until recent times. The civil economy tradition understands the whole of the economy and society as a matter of cooperation and reciprocity. The family company (still ninety per cent of the private sector in Italy), cooperatives and Adriano Olivetti can all be explained by taking seriously the cooperative and communal nature of the economy. This is why the European cooperative movement has been the most typical expression of the European market economy. For example, the Italian industrial districts of Prato (spun goods), Fermo (shoes) and Carpi (knitted goods) are entire communities that turned economic without ceasing to be communities. Thus while American capitalism has the anonymous market as its model and seeks to merchandise the firm, which is increasingly seen as a nexus of contracts, as a commodity or as a market with internal suppliers and clients, the European model has instead sought to "communitize" the market, taking the mutualistic and communal economy as its model, exporting it from the firm to the whole of civil life (that is, cooperation in credit and consumption). In so doing the latter takes on the costs and benefits of such an operation: an economy more full of humanity and love of life, but also of the wounds that are an inevitable part of human encounters.

The American model and its economic theory has now colonized the furthermost parts of the European economy and its economic tradition. This was partly because Europe's communal and cooperative tradition has not always worked as well as it could on the cultural and practical levels, and it did not develop in every region. Moreover, in Italy it has had to come to terms with the trauma –

not yet fully worked through – that in corporatism fascism declared itself as the true heir of the tradition of the cooperative firm and the medieval tradition of the arts and trades. However, the great crisis we are living through indicates that an economy and society based on cooperation without contact can create monsters, and that business that is just business in the end becomes anti-business. The ethos of the West is an interweaving of strong and weak forms of cooperation, including individuals who flee the bonds of community in search of freedom and people who freely bond together in order to live well. In a phase of history in which the global market is tending towards individuals without bonds, Europe must remember, preserve and live the intrinsically civil nature of the economy.

The recent economic and financial crisis is a marvellous test environment for what we have described. Beginning in the spring of 2007 in the United States, then spreading by contagion to Europe and elsewhere, the crisis was entropic by nature. It was neither a situational crisis nor a dialectical crisis. It was the culmination of a process that has been fundamentally modifying the way that finance works for over thirty years, to the point of undermining the very foundations of the liberal-democratic social order that has become the hallmark of Western civilization. We know that a crisis that emerges from a serious conflict of interests in a given society is dialectical in nature, but it contains within itself the seeds or forces to overcome it. Famous historical examples of such crises were the American Revolution (1765–83), the French Revolution (1789–99) and the October 1917 revolution in Russia. An entropic crisis, however, is one that originates from a conflict of values that tends to make the system collapse by implosion, with no indication within itself of a way out of it. This type of crisis develops whenever a society loses its bearings, its direction. The fall of the Roman Empire, the transition from feudalism to modernity, the fall of the

Berlin Wall and the consequent sunset of the Soviet empire are all notable historical examples.

Why is this distinction important? Because the exit strategies are different for dialectical and entropic crises. Although necessary, a society cannot exit an entropic crisis merely by making technical adjustments or by legislative and regulatory measures; it must face head-on the question of direction.[2] For this reason it is not right to equate the current crisis – except in its merely quantitative aspects – to the 1929 Great Depression, which was of a dialectic nature. This is not just because the "financialization" of the economy did not yet exist – it was not until the early 1980s that incipient globalization started that process – but primarily because the dual separation of work from wealth creation, and the market from democracy, that prompted the loss of direction in the current crisis was not yet complete. For centuries humanity held to the idea that work, in one form or another, was the source of wealth. It was no accident that Adam Smith opened his foundational work, *The Wealth of Nations* (1776) with just such a proposition. With the financialization of the economy has come the idea that speculative finance creates much more wealth, and far more quickly, than productive labour. The explosion in the number of university research programmes in business studies at the expense of other areas and the choice of study tracks and degree programmes by students enrolled in economics schools is evidence of how widely it has taken hold. The assertion and expansion of the financial ethos have validated, with

---

2. This is why prophetic minorities can be indispensable. By thinking outside accepted norms, and above all through the witness of what they do, they may indicate a new direction for a society. That is what happened when the father of Western monasticism, Benedict initiated his famous phrase *ora et labora*: he inaugurated the new era of cathedrals. With Benedict, work, considered for centuries a traditional activity of slaves, became the noble path to liberty: we work to be free.

the complicity of the media, the conviction that one need not work to become rich in a hurry; better to try one's luck, and above all without too many moral scruples. It is comforting to read what the American Nobel Laureate Robert Shiller wrote in his *Finance and the Good Society*:

> Errors by educators in recent decades seem to have played an important role in the severe financial crisis that began in 2007. In particular, the efficient markets theory was oversold to students, and this helped contribute to the formation of speculative bubbles. Many teachers seemed to inculcate the extreme view that markets are perfectly efficient. From this view many of their students drew the conclusion that it hardly matters ethically what one does in business, since nothing one could do would ever disturb this magnificent equilibrium.
>
> (Shiller 2012: 103)

Western civilization rests on a strong idea of the "good life", hence the right and obligation for everyone to plan their lives in view of *civil happiness*. But what is the starting point to attain such a goal, if not from work understood as the place for a good life? Human flourishing – *eudaimonia* in the Aristotelian sense – cannot be sought *after* work, as happened previously, because a person encounters her humanity *while* she works. This is why it is urgent to begin elaborating a concept of work that on the one hand surpasses the excessive increase in work that is typical of our time – work that fills a growing anthropological vacuum – and on the other that values articulating the idea of liberty *of* work – the liberty to choose the activities that can enrich the mind and heart of those engaged in work. This means that we must move from the idea of work as activity towards the idea of work as endeavour. Accepting such an idea of work implies that the goals of a company – whatever legal form it might take – are not reducible to profit alone, though without excluding it. This implies that companies with a civil vocation can emerge and develop and are able to transcend their own self-referentiality, broadening the space of effective possibilities for people to choose their own work.

The second separation at the root of the current crisis sets the market and democracy against each other. Economic theory – particularly the neo-Austrian school of thought – has always held that the success and progress of a society crucially depend on its ability to mobilize and manage the dispersed knowledge that exists among those who are part of it. Indeed, the main merit of the market, understood as a socio-economic institution, is precisely that of providing an optimal solution to the knowledge problem. As Friedrich von Hayek stated in his well-known 1937 essay *Economics and Knowledge*, a decentralized system of coordination is necessary in order to efficiently channel the local knowledge each citizen has in a society, and the price system that comprises the market is exactly what fits the need. This way of seeing things, which is very common among economists, nevertheless tends to obscure a point of central importance. The operation of the price system as a means of coordination presupposes that economic agents share, and thus understand, the "language" of the market. An analogy may help explain this. Pedestrians and drivers stop at a traffic light because they share the same meaning of the red light. If for some the red light evoked adherence to a particular political view, and for others it evoked a danger signal, it is clear that no coordination would be possible, with easily imaginable consequences. The example suggests that not one, but two types of knowledge are required in the market to attain the principal task described above. The first type resides in each individual and – as Hayek made clear – can be managed by normal market mechanisms. The second type of knowledge is the institutional knowledge that circulates among the various groups that make up a society, which has to do with the common language that allows a plurality of individuals to share the meanings of the discourse categories in use and to understand each other.

As the cultural sociologist Carlo Tognato has made clear, many different languages coexist, and the language of the market is but one of those. If the language of the market were the only one, there would be no problem: to efficiently mobilize the local knowledge of individuals, the usual market tools would suffice. But this is not the case, because contemporary societies are multicultural contexts in which individual knowledge must traverse linguistic boundaries, and from this formidable difficulties arise. Neo-Austrian thought was able to set aside that difficulty by implicitly assuming that the problem of institutional knowledge does not exist – for example, that all the members of a society share the same system of values and accept the same principles of social organization. But this is not the case; as is clear from reality, an institution other than the market is necessary to govern a "multi-linguistic" society so a language can emerge that can bring the members of different linguistic communities into dialogue.

That institution is the well-known model of deliberative democracy. The problem of knowledge management in today's societies – in short the problem of development – postulates that two institutions, democracy and the market, can cooperate side by side. Instead, the separation between the market and democracy that has been eroding over the course of the last quarter century, on a wave exalting a particular cultural relativism and an exacerbated individualistic mentality, has made us think – even informed scholars – that it was possible to expand the reach of the market without worrying about coming to terms with the necessity of expanding the forms of democracy. Exalting the merits of the market, narrow conformist thinking reached the conclusion that the world is what markets make it to be, and no citizen, not even governments, should have the power to correct its course.

We are persuaded that a significant benefit the civil economy paradigm brings about is precisely that of helping us reintegrate these two separations. It would be good were that to happen soon, because there are too many innocent people paying for the hubris of those who insist on believing in the self-referentiality of finance – when finance becomes an end in and of itself, and thus claims to be able to work without questions of direction. As the mythic tradition and Greek thought explain, the *phthónos theón*, the malevolence of the gods, is the response to hubris; that its consequences always fall on the least able and the most vulnerable is shamefully scandalous.

2

The cornerstones: Antonio Genovesi and Giacinto Dragonetti

Homo homini lupus. [Man to Man is an arrant Wolfe.]
— Thomas Hobbes, *De Cive*, 1642

Homo homini natura amicus. [Man is by nature a friend to man.]
— Antonio Genovesi, 1749

Antonio Genovesi (1713–69) is the best-known writer on the civil economy. And for good reason: he linked his principal work, *Lezioni di economia civile* (*Lessons of Civil Economy*, 1765–70) to the expression "civil economy". In Italy and other Latin countries, and in Germany as well, he represented a universal point of reference for the school of civil economy. He was also noted for his creativity, and for having been appointed in 1754 to the Chair of Commerce and Mechanics (i.e. civil economy), instituted by the Tuscan reformer Bartolomeo Intieri, at the University of Naples. We will not associate him with a particular pillar of the civil economy as we will with other authors in the following chapters, because he was "everyone's teacher".

It was in this same reformist context that Ferdinando Galiani (1728–87) published *Della Moneta* (*On Money*) in 1751, one of the most original and important works in eighteenth-century Europe, and which helped to raise Genovesi's profile as an economist. In fact, Genovesi was entrusted with the first chair of economics in Europe for which we have any trace; Intieri desired and financed the chair on condition that Genovesi be appointed to it and that the lessons be in Italian, which was itself a specific educational and reformist choice. A chair actually entitled Chair of Civil Economy was also instituted in Modena in 1772. Francesco III d'Este, Duke of Modena, appointed Agostino Paradisi to it; he was a more multi-faceted figure than simply an economist. The manuscript of his *Lezioni* (*Lessons*), which is clearly derived from Genovesi, is preserved in the Library of Modena and Reggio Emilia; their value awaits rediscovery. Sometimes unintended consequences bring good results, as illustrated with Genovesi's expulsion from the field of theology: he devoted the last fifteen years of his life almost exclusively to economics, ethics and anthropology, and his teachings became recognized throughout Enlightenment Europe.

In 1754 Genovesi published *Discorso sopra il vero fine delle lettere e delle scienze* (*Discourse on the True Purpose of the Letters and Sciences*), an analysis of the causes and reasons for the economic and civil decline of the Kingdom of Naples, a work which even today fully retains its force of thought and culture. Between 1765 and 1769 Genovesi published his most significant works, the most important of which was the *Lezioni di economia civile* (*Lessons of Civil Economy*), published in three editions, two in Naples and one in Milan, between 1765 and 1770, as a development of his 1757 work *Elementi di commercio* (*Elements of Commerce*). The manuscripts are preserved at the Biblioteca Nazionale di Napoli. These are now published in the first part of the critical edition of the *Lezioni di commercio o sia di economia civile* (*Lessons of Commerce or Civil*

Economy; Genovesi [1769] 2005). After publication, the *Lezioni* were immediately translated into German and Spanish. *Logica* (*Logic*) and *Diceosina o sia della filosofia del giusto e dell'onesto* (*Diceosina, or the Philosophy of the Just and the Honest*) followed in 1766. He annotated a new Italian translation of Montesquieu's *Esprit des lois* (*Spirit of the Laws*), which was published posthumously and incomplete in 1777. He died in Naples on 12 September 1769.

Genovesi wrote his economic treatise, *Lezioni di commercio o sia di economia civile* (*Lessons of Commerce or Civil Economy*), in Enlightenment Naples at the height of its cultural splendour. The very title of the Chair of Commerce and Mechanics that he held is also important; it emphasizes a central aspect of the generation of Neapolitan and Italian reformers of which Genovesi was a part, that of knowing how to link the economic and broader academic cultures to the practical applications necessary for creating a civil society. For medieval artisans, Leonardo, Torricelli and Intieri, Italy was (and still is) capable of civil and economic development when it brought practical and intellectual knowledge together, when speculative thought served life and people's well-being.

As it was for the Civic Humanists, Franciscans and Dominicans, for Genovesi the market was a matter of *philia*, or civil friendship. In his *Logica* we find an interesting link between his anthropology and rewards:

> Politics must make the people who make up the State into the densest, tightest body possible. This body is formed by studying the laws in order to firmly maintain the proportional mean between *concentrative* and *diffusive* forces, the two primitive forces of the human heart. But that proportional mean cannot be maintained except through immediate, clear and appropriate penalties for crimes, and through prompt, public rewards for great virtues.   (Genovesi 1766b: 322)

Because Genovesi's anthropology was based on an equilibrium of these two forces, he knew that if the diffusive force ("the love of the species") was not adequately cultivated, the concentrative force ("self-love"; Genovesi 1766a: 17) will grow excessively and damage both individuals and society: "The concentrative force often overpoweringly draws towards itself, resulting in a weakening of the diffusive force, which destroys the basis of the concentrative force itself" (*ibid.*: 19). At the same time, Genovesi knew that excessive growth of the love of the species produces imbalances, since "in doing too much good for others it kills itself, thus its efficacy ceases" (*ibid.*). In a note he added: "All those who were excessively zealous of the public good turned out badly. This is the continual story of Europe over three thousand years. All of its heroes died violently" (ibid.). With his views that sociality is natural rather than artificial, and that it has an essential role for a fully human and happy life, Genovesi is perfectly in line with the virtue ethics of the ancient Aristotelian and Thomist tradition.

However, if we get to the heart of the vision of life in community as seen by the Neapolitan school of civil economy, we immediately notice that for these authors (not just for Genovesi) "simple" sociality – being a human "political animal" – is insufficient for qualifying the human dimension with respect to other animals. The typical sociality of human beings is a *qualified* sociality, which we should call reciprocity, friendship and mutual assistance or fraternity; in the language of Genovesi and other authors of the tradition, these expressions are essentially synonyms:

> It is a common saying that humans are naturally sociable animals. But not everyone believes that there are any animals that are not sociable. ... In what then should we say that humans are more sociable than other animals? ... [It is the]

reciprocal right of being assisted, and consequently the reciprocal obligation to assist each other in our needs.

(Genovesi [1769] 2005: ch. 1, paras 16–17)

In this passage there is something we do not find in either Aristotle
or Adam Smith: for Genovesi, *reciprocity* – not just relationality or
simple sociality – is the typical element of human sociality. Rather,
for Smith, what constitutes the typical element of human relationality is the tendency to truck, barter and exchange, based, as
we have seen, on the capacity of persuasion. Nor does Genovesi
embrace the anthropological theory, as did the Neoplatonist Third
Earl of Shaftesbury (1671–1713), that humans by nature are altru-
istic; it was important for Genovesi to emphasize reciprocity over
altruism. Genovesi saw economic relations in the market as relationships of mutual assistance; they were neither impersonal nor
anonymous. Indeed, the market itself is conceived as an expression
of reciprocity as the general law of civil society. His theory of reciprocity, seen as a fundamental law of human relations, derives from
a sort of moral Newtonian system, which inspired his scientific
vision. Following Francis Hutcheson, one of the founding fathers of
the Scottish Enlightenment, he associated the law of gravity discov-
ered by Newton with the idea of reciprocity, since the law indicates
a mutual attraction between bodies that decreases with "social"
distance. That is evident and important, above all in his analysis of
trust, or "public faith" that is at the heart of his *Lezioni*.

The market is mutual assistance

Understanding Genovesi's vision of economic life requires that we
begin from his anthropological and ethical theories; rather than
placing familiar words such as "money", "population" and "luxury"

at the heart of the system, we must instead use words such as "trust", "mutual advantage" and "happiness". Let us begin with *trust*. As it was for the Franciscans of the fourteenth and fifteenth centuries, for Genovesi the market was a matter of trust – *fides*. A key expression in Genovesi's civil economy was in fact "public faith", which is the real precondition of economic development: confidence is the soul of commerce. There is a substantial difference in his thought between *private* trust (which is one's reputation, a private good that can be "spent" in the market) and *public* trust, which although not the sum of private reputations, does include a genuine love for the common good. It is a concept similar to what modern social theorists call "social capital", that is, the fabric of trust and civil virtues that make it possible for human and economic development to begin and sustain over time. This is why Ludovico Bianchini, a follower of Genovesi nearly a century later, emphasized that public faith is not just a means, it is also "part of the wealth" of a nation (Bianchini 1855: 21). For Genovesi it was exactly the lack of "public faith" that explained the lack of civil and economic development in the Kingdom of Naples – an analysis that after two centuries has lost none of its relevance.

According to the civil economy tradition, in Naples there was an abundance of "private trust" (understood as particular social bonds linked to blood ties or feudal vassalage pacts), but little public trust emerging from civil virtues. A few decades later Gaetano Filangieri (1752–88) was also convinced of this. In his view there could be no civil and economic development without "confidence in the government, confidence in the magistrates and confidence in other citizens" (Filangieri [1780] 2003: 5), which are the primary and principal resources for any type of collective and individual development. If it is true that developing markets also brings civil and economic development, for the Neapolitan school of thought it is even more urgent to emphasize that the *cultivation* of public faith is the precondition for any discussion about economic and civil development: "Nothing is more necessary than public faith for a broad and ready circulation [of goods]" (Genovesi [1769] 2005: 751). Something Genovesi specified in a note is important: "This word *fides* means a cord that binds and unites. Public faith is thus the bond of families united in a sociable life" (*ibid.*).

His attention to the ethical dimension of civil life led him to write several important works, primarily the *Diceosina* (an Italianization of the Greek word *dikaiosyne*, or "justice"), on the primitive rights of humans, which places him among the founders of the human rights tradition, certainly in the Latin countries.

> Every inborn property of humans, either of body or of soul, is an *usia*, a *jus*, an innate right of humans. ... Life, limb, liberty and the inborn forces of the soul and body are rights that are born with us; a piece of ground taken from the mother community and cultivated for use as one's livelihood, domesticated wild animals, and so forth are legitimately acquired rights: everything that comes to us through just covenants and contracts is by right transmitted to us.
>
> (Genovesi 1766a: 16–17)

Furthermore, he added a right that today would be called (by authors such as Amartya Sen) a social right, the right to mutual aid: "Preserve the rights of everyone intact: rather, support those rights as much as you know how and are able" (*ibid.*: 21). Further on he specified that:

> Among the rights of our nature is not just that of being secure in one's property, which is a *perfect right*, but also that of being a person assisted by another person in one's needs, that of reciprocal aid, which is an imperfect right, "seemingly because others cannot be forced to offer it to us".   (Genovesi 1766a)

In a note he added:

> This is the idea as it exists in civil societies, in which this right
> is rarely made a matter of law since the [possible] outcomes
> are limitless, hence in most cases it cannot become law or
> a moral principle. In nature, however, it has a function as
> perfect as *jus* itself, since inhumanity and cruelty are as far
> off the path to happiness as is iniquity. ... The Gospel made
> it the soul of Christian law, such that the reasons for eternal
> life or death in the decree of the last judgement in Matthew
> 25 were about the observance or the neglect of the right of
> assistance.   (Genovesi 1766a: 38)

These statements contain the crux of Genovesi's philosophy of the
civil economy and his vision of the market as "mutual assistance"
and a space for reciprocity.

Public happiness

The theme of happiness is central to Genovesi's work and a pillar of
the entire Italian tradition of the civil economy. There is indeed a
profound relationship between economics and happiness, though
partly unexpected and unstated. Modern economics emerged in
several Italian city-states as the science of "public happiness". The
cultural reference of the social research during this period, which
was directly connected to Civic Humanism, is the Aristotelian and
Thomist tradition. According to this tradition, happiness is *after*
the virtues, since happiness is their meaning and fulfilment. For
Aristotle, civil life, including the *agora* and the market, is also a
place for the practice of the virtues, and thus happiness, as long
as the market does not become unnaturally chrematistic, in which

wealth is sought as an end in itself and not simply as a means for living well. In Genovesi's writings there are a few "maxims and first truths" relative to morality, among which are these: "That one must thus be virtuous to be happy; that we are capable of virtue, and that this virtue is not a vain and chimeric voice, but true and real" (Genovesi 1758: 2). Civil economy and public happiness are thus two key concepts in the Italian Enlightenment movement (and in a certain sense in the European Enlightenment), although in Italy the meanings and emphases were different in the various cities, and even within any one city.

Civil economy (Naples), political economy (Milan), public economy (Milan) and national economy (Venice) are all adjectives that first stated a common trait throughout the whole of the reformist eighteenth century, and only later indicated regional or national differentiations. This common trait highlighted a radical departure from Aristotelian and ancient economics, where the law of the *oikos* (house, thus *oikos-nomos*) ended where politics, the law of the *polis*, the city, began. The *oikos* was based essentially on blood ties and hierarchy, and the polis on *philia*, or friendship, among peers.

Economics, whether civil, public, social or national, indicates that the nature and laws of this science leave aside the household and community in order to focus on the national dimension, on the wealth of the *nations* or on *public* happiness. Furthermore – and here Italy is truly in company with the principal thinkers of the European Enlightenment such as Hume, Kant, Montesquieu and Smith – the development of markets and commerce is an essential vehicle for public happiness. Government and "good principles" play an important role in increasing the public happiness of the people, as the Italian historian Ludovico Antonio Muratori (1672–1750) expressed in the subtitle of his treatise *Della pubblica felicità, oggetto de' buoni principi* (*On Public Happiness, the Goal of Good Principles*).

Contemporary perspectives on public happiness were derived from the legacies of Aristotle and Aquinas, and of Cicero (particularly in Dragonetti), Civic Humanism, Rousseau, Montesquieu and Vico, in the Neapolitan civil economy, sensism in Milan, as well as others. Moreover, happiness is a familiar word in modernity, used in a very particular way in the Italian, French and Spanish Enlightenments of Latin origin. Public happiness even became a sort of slogan among eighteenth-century Italian economists, a "chrism" of the Italian economics tradition, that endured until the nineteenth century, and which is being revived today. Achille Loria (whom we will soon consider), restating a theme that was common knowledge at the time in Italy, wrote that "All our economists are concerned less with the *wealth of nations*, as was [Adam] Smith, than with *public happiness*" (Loria 1904: 85).

So, while Protestant humanism in the United States posited the right to the "pursuit of happiness" as central, at the same time in Naples the right and duty of public happiness was affirmed. That message is even more central today: it reminds us that the most important happiness is not our own, but rather that of all, and especially that of children.

Giacinto Dragonetti: rewarding virtues

As we've already mentioned there is a close link between the civil economy and the virtues. An idea originating in the Aristotelian and Thomist tradition is that virtue is stronger and more deeply rooted than vice. The dominance of virtue over vice is what makes it reasonable to offer rewards, at least equal in number and measure to punishments. With its deep Reformed and Lutheran origins, modernity represents an anthropological – and thus ethical – shift: the idea that humanity is capable of good and of virtue has been eclipsed to the point that we must be content with self-interest and the invisible hand.

Although remaining open to modern authors, the civil economy tradition in Italy attempted to remain anchored in virtue ethics and the concept of the common good. The author who took the theme of the virtues most seriously was Giacinto Dragonetti (1738–1818). From an ancient and noble family of L'Aquila, he first went to Rome to study, then to Naples in 1760, where he dedicated himself to jurisprudence and became a student of Genovesi. In 1766 he wrote a brief treatise called *Delle virtù e de' premi* (*On Virtues and Rewards*). The title was somewhat unfortunate, because it was essentially a marketing choice by the bookseller to launch the book in the wake of the well-known European Enlightenment bestseller, *Dei delitti e delle pene* (*On Crimes and Punishments*), published by his contemporary Cesare Beccaria just two years earlier (both were published anonymously).

Just as Pietro Verri (1728–97) and the Il Caffè group were behind the young Beccaria's *Dei delitti e delle pene*, it is highly probable that Genovesi and Bartolomeo Intieri's *Accademia delle scienze* (Academy of the Sciences) were behind the young Dragonetti's book. It is also probable that the title was suggested to him by Gravier, the publisher, or by Genovesi himself, because, as has recently become clear with the publication of several letters from Dragonetti to his brother, when the book was nearly finished he had not yet read the work by "Beccheria", as he called him in a letter. Dragonetti soon left research to enter the judiciary, where he attained the highest responsibilities. He completed only a second volume on the origins of the Sicilian fiefdoms in 1788, in which he continued his battle against feudal institutions. That battle led him to participate in the 1799 Neapolitan Revolution; he was exiled in France, where he remained for several years. In the introduction to *Delle virtù e de' premi* we read: "Men have made millions of laws to punish crimes, and they have not established even one to reward virtues" (Dragonetti 1766: 3). Actually, the theme of rewards was present, though not central, in Beccaria's *Dei delitti e delle pene*.

The main idea of Dragonetti's *Delle virtù e de' premi* attributes an essential role to "rewards" for virtues, or a *virtue ethic*. It is thus anti-Hobbesian and aligned with an Aristotelian and Thomist view; from this point of view it is also aligned with the Roman republican tradition – of Cicero and Plutarch, for example – and partially with the Lockean tradition. But how should one reward virtues? It is immediately clear that rewarding virtue cannot be something similar to what today is called an "incentive". In fact, an incentive is a punishment with a minus sign, and it has the same extrinsic nature and purpose: obtain something from someone who would not do it spontaneously or sincerely. In which case, what is a reward for virtue in Dragonetti's thought? Even prior to that though, how does Dragonetti understand virtue? He associates it with directly and intentionally seeking the common good (as distinct from a private good, and not necessarily aligned with it).

Dragonetti described civil society and its construction similarly to Locke and Rousseau: the human person is by nature sociable and loving, but resource scarcities and disordered passions produce conflicts, and from these the social contract and its related laws emerge. When someone acts towards another's advantage, we are dealing with virtues: "The name virtue is given to all actions that regard others' interests, or to the preference for others' good over one's own good" (Dragonetti 1766: 7). It is thus clear that for Dragonetti seeking one's personal interest, although natural, is not virtuous action. Virtue requires effort and sacrifice:

> We call God good more than we call him virtuous, because he need not force himself to do good ... Virtue is none other than a generous effort, independently of law, that leads us to

be useful to others. Its extremes are the sacrifice or detriment
of the virtuous person and its resulting public usefulness.
(Dragonetti 1766: 7)

So one necessary condition for virtue is sacrifice and effort; the
other element or sufficient condition is public utility, or the public
good. He added: "Many mistakenly give the name virtue to actions
that are a pure effect of natural, divine or civil law, for which a more
proper word would be duties" (*ibid.*: 8). In the first half of the nineteenth century Melchiorre Gioia (1767–1829) was the sole Italian
writer to take up Dragonetti's theme in his work *Del merito e delle
ricompense: Trattato storico e filosofico* (*On Merit and Recompense:
A Historical and Philosophical Treatise*). Recognizing Dragonetti's
primacy, he added two more elements beyond sacrifice and usefulness: disinterestedness in the result and social convenience, which
were quite present in Dragonetti's work. So now the distinction
between reward and incentive became clear: incentives aim at
private good, while rewards are linked to the public good.

Rewards, not just incentives

In *Delle virtù e de' premi* Dragonetti wrote:

Since virtue is not a product of the command of law, but
rather of our free will, society has no right over it whatsoever. Virtue in no way enters in the social contract; if it is left
unrewarded, society commits an injustice similar to cheating
another of his sweat [labour]. (Dragonetti 1766: 11–12)

Thus a reward is a recompense for an action that goes beyond contracts and laws; it is a recompense for an essentially gratuitous act.

It is true that all members of the state owe it the services commanded by law, but it is also beyond doubt that citizens should be individuated and rewarded in proportion to their *gratuitous services*. The virtues are the many considerable and arbitrary services offered to the state. The virtues that are more than human are those that are *sufficient in themselves*.

(Dragonetti 1766: 12, emphasis added)

The expressions "gratuitous services" and "sufficient in themselves" reveal a key ingredient of a theory of civil virtues: the recompense of virtues is virtue itself. Thus, even though society must in some way reward virtues from the outside, the external recompense depends on and is complementary to the primary form of remuneration, which is intrinsic and internal to the virtuous person. In other words, education and *culture* are required so that a virtue ethic might operate and expand in society. But immediately afterwards, as one might have expected, Dragonetti raised a question crucial to the discussion of rewarding virtues: "Nor should one find reason to object that when compensation is proposed for virtues, they will be seen as mercenary and no longer generous actions" (*ibid.*). How might this happen? How can we offer compensation for civil virtues such that the "external" reward not transform the gratuitousness of virtue into a commercial exchange, which would entail the loss of the spontaneity and liberty that is typical of virtue? Dragonetti did not actually present a well-formed theory on this, but he did point out several interesting insights that express Genovesi's general vision of the civil economy, in which there is no opposition between the various forms of reciprocity, or between virtue and self-interest.

First of all, he stated that love for the common good does not diverge from self-love. Referring to the times of the Roman Republic and the Greek *polis*, Dragonetti wrote that "public greatness was not confined to a few, rather, it was so widespread among the citizens that public interests were confused with private interests. The republicans, while seemingly sacrificing themselves for their country, were serving their own advantage" (Dragonetti 1766: 13–14). His definition of reward follows from that: "A reward is the necessary bond linking individual interest with the general interest, and to keep people always focused on the good. Hence the Virtues, which per the social contract do not appertain to society, should not remain cheated of the reward due them" (*ibid.*: 14–15). The rest of Dragonetti's pamphlet is replete with important points, such as the one on commerce previously cited. The conclusion is worth stating: "The happiest State is the one in which precedence is measured by virtue" (*ibid.*: 102). The central part of the book lists several criteria for correctly relating rewards and virtues, to avoid high recompense going to acts of little virtue (and of little use to society) and little recompense going to actions of high virtue, since "one does greater harm by badly placing recompense than by suppressing it" (*ibid.*: 19).

Thus a reward does not coincide with what today we call an "incentive": a reward recognizes virtue; it does not create it. An incentive, which is wholly extrinsic, creates the incentivized behaviour that would not happen without the incentive, and it stops when the incentive ends. Every organization or community that wants to develop its members' virtues must reduce incentives and increase rewards. For the practical relevance of the distinction between incentives and rewards in economic applications, it can be helpful to highlight the basic differences between the two categories.

First, a principal in a certain relationship of agency induces her agent to act in the *private* interest of the principal: consider the relationship between a company and its directors, or between an organization and its close partners, or between a parent and child. In other words, the ultimate goal of the incentive scheme is to align the agent's interest with that of the principal. In the case of a company, this means assuming that the personal interest of the administrator–agent coincides with that of the shareholders for whom he acts. Rewards are not like this because, as stated, they aim at the common good.

Second, the formal structure of incentives is that of a contract that, once agreed to by both parties in a relationship of agency, becomes binding on both, even though it is always possible for the agent to manipulate the incentives. Incentives are thus *ex ante* with respect to action, in the sense that the contractual terms must be known to the agent before she sets herself to work. Rewards on the contrary are *ex post*, since they are a voluntary act by the principal who, as principal, does not establish a prior obligation on the parties. The essence of a reward is thus that of a gift, while the essence of an incentive is attributing to the agent part of the added value he creates. In the long run the practice of incentives, on a wide scale and across many settings of social life, will weaken and "crowd out" the spirit of gift in a community.

Third, one of the most undesired effects of incentives is the erosion of the relationship of trust between the principal and the agent. Consider any example of a contract with incentives: sooner or later it is inevitable that the agent asks himself why his principal is offering him the incentive. It will be one or the other of these cases: if what is asked of the agent is within what is specified in the work contract, offering an incentive constitutes the price that the principal is prepared to pay for his lack of confidence in the moral integrity of the agent. If instead the agent is asked to do more than the provisions of the contract, or something that violates the commercial ethical code, then the incentive is either a partial exploitation of the agent's extra effort, or a payment to induce the agent to overcome her moral resistance, which today is the more common. (One need only consider the incentive of granting stock options to the managers of large financial firms to induce them to do what they would never do otherwise.) In both cases, the result is a loss of the agent's self-esteem, about which Adam Smith wrote in the *Theory of Moral Sentiments* (1759). If a bank manager, in order to claim an incentive, deceives a client who asks her advice on buying financial products, she loses her self-esteem and ultimately her own spiritual well-being – and above all her trust capital is eroded. And, as we know, without trust no one can survive in a market economy. None of this happens with rewards, which, by increasing self-esteem, reinforces social bonds.

Whether little or much, incentives always create dependence. The Latin *incentivus* derives from *incinere*, which means to "enchant"; the Latin peoples had already understood that the nature of incentives is to bedazzle. This is why incentives are inflationary: one need only look at the compensation of today's top managers compared to that of a few decades ago. Additionally, incentives lower the psychological costs of temptation; this is why they create adverse effects. Rewards are not like that; rather, they function to point out notable individual characteristics that are not otherwise observable, such as passion, loyalty, group spirit, and so forth.

Against all rents

It is a well-known fact that the malady of the Italian system is the culture of rent-seeking; this is due to myriad historical reasons, among them a distorted relationship with the state and a paternalism inadequately fought by the Catholic Church. The parasitic tendency towards rents leads people to extract income not from active money flows, but from previously acquired privileges and rights. Achille Loria knew this well, as we shall see. Today, as well as in the Kingdom of Naples, this parasitic tendency was favoured by what Genovesi might have called today "can't-do-it-itis": "But that 'can't do it', which first emerged from the weakness of the judges and was later strengthened by greed, has ruined the most admirable laws" (Genovesi [1769] 2005: 155).

Dragonetti developed his anti-feudal polemic in his second work, *Sull'origine dei feudi* (*On the Origins of Fiefs*, 1788). Feudal society did not produce wealth, and thus civil development, because compensation was based on acquired privileges rather than on virtue. This is a stance that has lost none of its revolutionary force over a span of two and a half centuries.

Praise for commerce and the arts emerged from his anti-feudal polemic, but this can only be understood correctly in relation to the entire Neapolitan Enlightenment project: to construct a post-feudal society that, thanks to the proper recompense for true virtues, would launch a new phase of civil life. This is why Dragonetti's cultural discourse, like that of Genovesi and Filangieri, was a *direct* discourse on the market and a theory of economic development, not a moral or merely juridical discourse. How might we then envision rewarding virtues as a path to civil and economic development? In general, the aim of the educational and reformational work by Genovesi, Dragonetti and Filangieri was trying to teach students to "sincerely" love the virtues, attributing intrinsic value to them, and to show them that virtue has its own logic and rationality, particularly when it is reciprocal (as Genovesi noted); this was a common thread running through the entire civil economy tradition. Dragonetti's juridical and political arguments are along the same lines, to find mechanisms that can "reward" virtue, but in such a way that they reward rather than crowd out virtues. Giacomo Leopardi understood this well when in his 1824 work *Discorso sopra lo stato presente dei costumi degli italiani* (*Discourse on the Present State of the Manners of the Italians*) he wrote:

> The restraints of laws and public force, which now seem
> to be the only ones remaining on society, have long been

recognized as highly insufficient to hold back evil, and even more to stimulate good. Everyone knows, along with Horace, that laws without customs are not enough.

(Leopardi [1824] 1906: 338)

Just as the market is not opposed to civil society, for Dragonetti rewarding virtue is not opposed to normal market remunerations, as long as these are just and civil. Dragonetti's book had good success in eighteenth-century Europe (and in Poland and Russia as well): it was published in Venice, Modena and Palermo, as well as in French and English. It was cited contentiously (and one understands why) by the English philosopher and jurist, Jeremy Bentham and his followers, and enthusiastically in America by Thomas Paine in his 1776 work *Common Sense*. There were several reprintings of both his books in the first half of the nineteenth century, after which it passed into oblivion. Today the theme of rewarding virtuous behaviour is seeing renewed interest, even though the culture of incentives is still dominant. Dragonetti and his great but forgotten theme of rewards is still awaiting rediscovery and re-evaluation.

One practical consequence of Dragonetti's argument is worth mentioning briefly. We know that there are three types of norms that a society needs in order to progress and have a future. First, there are *legal* norms that are an expression of the coercive power of the state, the enforceability of which is assured by sanction – that is, by punishment. Second, there are *social* norms that are the result of conventions and traditions that say something about the history of that society; their enforceability depends on shame, social stigma and the loss of status subsequent to their violation. Finally, there are *moral* norms associated with well-defined cultural origins that identify a society; violating them creates a sense of guilt in the transgressor. The distinction between a shame culture and a guilt culture is attributable to the American anthropologist Ruth Benedict (author of *The Chrysanthemum and the Sword*), who stated that the transition from the former to the latter historically represented real progress. This is because, as the philosopher Bernard Williams explained in *Shame and Necessity*, "The most primitive experiences of shame are connected with sight and being seen, but it has been interestingly suggested that guilt is rooted in hearing, the sound in oneself of the voice of judgement" (Williams 1993: 89). So, if a society's laws are not congruent with its social and moral norms, the former never produce the desired results, as history confirms. The fact is that a social order requires that all three types of norms proceed in the same direction if one wants to guarantee that they are credible and acceptable. Recently, American jurisprudence coined the term *inexpressive laws* to denote those laws that do not express the values and ethos of a people. The outcome is visible to all: inexpressive laws are not respected, or they require preparing costly and frequently counterproductive incentive schemes to make them respected. This point helps us understand why laws that work well in one country do not have the same results when transplanted to another in which the social and moral norms are different.

The eclipse of the civil economy

Genovesi and the civil economy did not enter the mainstream of economic thought in the nineteenth and twentieth centuries, even in Italy, where the judgement pronounced against it by Francesco Ferrara (1810–1900), the most influential Italian economist of the nineteenth century, was quite negative. In the introduction of the third volume of the first series of his famous *Biblioteca dell'economista* (*Economist's Library*), he wrote regarding eighteenth-century Italian economists (even though he recognized Genovesi as first among them): "The merit for the foundations of economics belong to the English Smith, or to the French Turgot, rather than to Genovesi, Verri, or Beccaria" (Ferrara 1852: xxxvi). The true economic science was sought outside of Italy, rather than among the Italian classics. The generation of economists after Ferrara – Maffeo Pantaleoni and Vilfredo Pareto – continued to look outside Italy (certainly Pareto) rather than to the civil economy tradition. It did not disappear, however. It survived as a sort of subterranean current of Italian and other economists (some consciously, others as "healthy carriers") who in various ways carried forward the idea of economics as civilizing, tied to civil virtues (and not just self-interest), tied to public happiness (and not just the wealth of nations), and without forgetting the role of institutions (without becoming Hobbesian).

The civil economy tradition was taken forward not so much by theoretical economists, but by applied economists, political scientists, jurists and several Italian proponents of corporate economics. In a certain sense the creators of the Italian cooperative movement were the ones who most authentically carried forward Genovesi's and Dragonetti's economics. We have in mind Ugo Rabbeno, Vito Cusumano, Giuseppe Tovini, Luigi Luzzatti, Ghino Valenti, Loene Wollemborg, and the many others who founded rural banks and consumption and production cooperatives, constructing the civilizing economy theorized by Genovesi. Even today in Italy the civil economy lives on in social cooperation, fair and solidarity trade, the Economy of Communion, ethical banks, social enterprises and all the corporate forms that have internalized reciprocity and the civil virtues as their driving forces.

Genovesi died in 1769, when his system of economic thought was still in full development; at the time he was working on the third edition of his *Lezioni*. In a certain sense, his research project died with him. However, his work has its own completeness, particularly in these times of crisis in which the appeals for ethics in economics, and the need to imagine more social and less individualistic market virtues, are as urgent as they were in Genovesi's time:

> I am about to publish my *Lessons of Commerce* in two volumes. ... My purpose is to see if I might leave my Italians a little more enlightened than I found them when I arrived, as well as a little more favourable towards virtue, which alone can be the true mother of all good. It is useless to think of the arts, commerce or government unless one thinks about reforming morality. As long as people make their way in life as scoundrels, we should not expect much from methodological efforts. I have too much experience with this.
>
> (Genovesi 1963: 168)

3

Good wealth: John Ruskin

People in the West generally hold that the whole duty of man is to promote the happiness of the majority of mankind, and happiness is supposed to mean only physical happiness and economic prosperity. If the laws of morality are broken in the conquest of this happiness, it does not matter very much. Again, as the object sought to be attained is the happiness of the majority, Westerners do not think there is any harm if this is secured by sacrificing a minority. The consequences of this line of thinking are writ large on the face of Europe. This exclusive search for physical and economic well-being prosecuted in disregard of morality is contrary to divine law, as some wise men in the West have shown. One of these was John Ruskin who contends in *Unto This Last* that men can be happy only if they obey the moral law.

– M. K. Gandhi, "Unto This Last: A Paraphrase"[1]

---

1. These are the opening lines of the introduction of an English translation by Valji Govindji Desai of M. K. Gandhi's translation of Ruskin's work into Gujarati. An online version of the English translation is available at www.mkgandhi.org/untothislast/untothislast.htm (accessed March 2016).

The ideas of English social critic and reformer, John Ruskin (1819–1900) show elements of modernity and remarkable originality which, in contrast with many other critics of early capitalism, make reading his works both current and highly stimulating. This is particularly true of *Unto This Last*, his economic and social commentary magnum opus. We will consider two aspects of his thought from this book – the motives for work and wealth – which we consider particularly significant and prophetic for our present-day economy and society.

Ruskin was both a critic of capitalism – because of workers' conditions in factories – and a critic of the economic theory of his time, that of David Ricardo, Thomas Robert Malthus and particularly that of John Stuart Mill. Today he would have been even more critical of our capitalism and economic theory, which have exacerbated those vices he identified and stigmatized in his own generation. From this perspective Ruskin was on the side of the utopian socialists (like Robert Owen, he tried to constitute an ideal community of workers), Karl Marx, US President Andrew Johnson and, in Italy, Arturo Labriola, Achille Loria, Ugo Rabbeno and the many theorists of cooperation, as well as social Christians like Giuseppe Toniolo (the Gospels and the biblical tradition are essential background for understanding Ruskin's criticism of capitalism).

The first regards the motives that drive people to work, and particularly to work done well. With uncommon force and clarity, Ruskin delineated a crucial theme for our form of capitalism and for our companies. If after a century and a half his questions remain as crucial as they were in his time, either capitalism and its economic theory have failed to take them seriously, or they have intentionally discarded them because they are too difficult and uncomfortable to face. Ruskin was convinced that it was an error in economic theory – in Mill more than in Smith – to start from a human being that is motivated by the search for pleasure or selfish ends, while systematically and intentionally overlooking other motives in life.

Ruskin was interested in understanding capitalism in order to understand as well the anthropological dynamic of work in the factory. He clearly recognized that self-interest, or seeking one's own maximum gain, was one of the motivations of the worker, but he was also convinced that workers are far more complex than a machine that responds to only one incentive. He wrote:

But he being, on the contrary, an engine whose motive power is a Soul, the force of this very peculiar agent, as an unknown quantity, enters into all the political economists' equations, without his knowledge, and falsifies every one of their results. The largest quantity of work will not be done by this curious engine for pay, or under pressure, or by help of any kind of fuel which may be applied by the chaldron. It will be done only when the motive force, that is to say, the will or spirit of the creature, is brought to its greatest strength by its own proper fuel; namely, by the affections.   (Ruskin [1860] 1901: 10)

We had to wait for the work of psychologists such as Edward Deci and Richard Ryan in the 1970s, the recent work of sociologists like Norbert Alter and corporate economists like Anouk Grévin, for even a few economists today to begin to be aware that workers have a soul, that they are not "carrot and stick" machines, and that they are highly sensitive to signals of recognition, reciprocity and rewards – not just incentives. In the majority of textbooks today, neoclassical economics continues to teach that workers' goals are not aligned with employers' goals, and that the main way to align them is to incentivize workers to make them do things they would not otherwise do, but which they will do because they are subjects who work well if monitored and adequately paid. Ruskin, on the other hand, believed that honour and virtue can be as important as motivators in ordinary economic settings, including factories. Anticipating the response of the economists of his time (J. S. Mill, for example), he wrote:

"The social affections", says the economist, "are accidental and disturbing elements in human nature; but avarice and the desire of progress are constant elements. Let us eliminate the inconstants, and, considering the human being merely as a covetous machine, examine by what laws of labour, purchase, and sale, the greatest accumulative result in wealth is attainable. Those laws once determined, it will be for each individual afterwards to introduce as much of the disturbing affectionate element as he chooses, and to determine for himself the result on the new conditions supposed." (Ruskin [1860] 1901: 1–2)

And in fact, a few decades later Maffeo Pantaleoni (1857–1924), an Italian economist who was a good student of Mill, challenged Ruskin's heirs, the social economists of his time, to demonstrate that the reasons that drove

street sweepers to sweep the streets, the tailor to make a suit, the tram driver to put in twelve hours of service in a tram, the miller to buy and sell grain, the farmer to hoe the field, and so forth [are] honour, dignity, a spirit of sacrifice, the expectation of heavenly rewards, patriotism, love of one's neighbour, a spirit of solidarity, imitating their ancestors and for the good of their descendants [and not] just a sort of economic advantage. (Pantaleoni 1925: 217).

However, Giuseppe Toniolo, an economist contemporary with Pantaleoni, was on Ruskin's side (he too was marginalized from the mainstream in his day). A few years after *Unto This Last*, in an 1873 work entitled *Dell'elemento etico quale fattore intrinseco delle leggi economiche* (*On the Ethical Element as an Intrinsic Factor of Laws*) – later merged into *Trattato di economica sociale* (*Treatise on the Social Economy*) – Toniolo wrote:

> Indeed, a non-prejudicial analysis of the complex nature of the person identifies, along with the principle of utility, the principle of good, the product of a spontaneous recognition of a prevailing moral law, which engenders the awareness of duty: ... the religious spirit ..., the sentiment of honesty and of fairness that emanates from it; the worship of what is true and what is beautiful, which shares a common foundation with it; the habit of temperance and the virtue of sacrifice.
>
> (Quoted in Sorrentino 2012: 224)

Who is correct? Pantaleoni or Toniolo? Mill or Ruskin? Actually, the question should not be asked at the level of "reason" or "truth", but at the level of the power and success of economic theories. Everyone – economists, philosophers and intellectuals in general – knew that the two arguments were both plausible and reasonable. We know today that there was no necessary reason for political economy to take the Mill–Pantaleoni path, because there was no intrinsic force in the nature of things that would have taken science down that track rather than Ruskin's. The main reason lies instead within the specific events and power relationships that prevailed during that century and a half within the economics community, as well as in the broader community (business people, politicians and others) that sustained it and supported it financially as well. After 1918, the shift in the geopolitical centre of the world towards the United States contributed in no small measure to the decline of the German and Italian schools of thought, which proceeded along the methodological lines of Ruskin and Toniolo. Equally significant was the lack of great theoretical talent within the community of economists that could have presented a critical discourse with the same language and mathematical rigour of a Pareto and the English (John Hicks was the first) and American (Paul Samuelson) economists who followed him. Today that paradigm is buckling because the cultural climate has changed in the world; by now many critical economists – such as Amartya Sen – use the same language as well but to say different things on an anthropological and value-related level.

Among the other reasons for its success, there is one element worth emphasizing. That element is the Protestant Reformation and the anthropological turn it produced. The Reformation and Counter-Reformation offer extraordinary evidence of the power of unintended consequences. As we will see, beyond the intentions of Luther and other reformers, the humanism that began asserting itself in the second half of the sixteenth century in northern Europe, and then in the United States (where modern economic science flourishes, and not by accident) is characterized by a strong, Augustinian-influenced anthropological pessimism (as is known, Luther had been an Augustinian monk). The radical incapacity of the natural person for virtue – Adam's post-sin decline – produced a strong anthropological parsimony, which in those countries supplanted the medieval philosophy and theology, and in particular Thomist thought, that had produced, partly through strong Aristotelian influence, a naturally sociable anthropology.

The Hobbesian wolf-man emerged from Luther, not from Aquinas, from whom instead came Genovesi's *homo homini natura amicus* ("man is by nature the friend of man") in eighteenth-century Naples. Virtue ethics disappeared from the scene because it was unrealistic for a person fundamentally diseased by lust and greed. So, since virtue had to be rejected for constructing civil and commercial society, it was necessary to settle for the more bleak but realistic self-interest. Ruskin and a good many economists of Catholic origins during the nineteenth and twentieth centuries reacted against this bleakness and anthropological parsimony. Ruskin not only sustained this in principle, he presented evidence and logic to demonstrate that an economic agent (a "merchant") that is only egoistic does not and cannot exist, because life is far more rich and abundant than such a myopic and distorted vision of theory and practice.

Which wealth is good?

The second aspect of Ruskin's thought we want to emphasize regards wealth. In pages of elegant passages, with touches of colour, culture and intelligence, Ruskin first discusses that wealth is an easily defined primitive concept, then proceeds to offer a great many arguments to illustrate that wealth in and of itself not only says little about people's happiness and a good life, but says it badly, at times very badly. Anyone who knows a little about today's debate on gross domestic product (GDP) and well-being will find many points that reinforce and enrich his ideas. One of Ruskin's general themes, which constitutes the defining structure of his book, is that the art of "becoming rich", in the usual sense, is not just the art of accumulating a lot of money, but rather to do so in such a way that those around us have less: "In accurate terms, it is 'the art of establishing the maximum inequality in our own favour'" (Ruskin [1860] 1901: 48). At first glance the phrase might make one think that Ruskin had fallen prey to the mercantilist fallacy (that exchange is a zero-sum game, that is, if one becomes wealthier another becomes poorer), but his reasoning is more complex. His insight, which has its origin in Smith's concept of "commanded labour", consists in maintaining that wealth is desired when it can command the action, or labour, of people who have less or no wealth. According to Ruskin, in a world without inequality, in which everyone is equally wealthy (or perhaps equally poor), there would be no incentive to work for others in exchange for wealth.

The market economy thus has a structural requirement of inequality:

> What is really desired, under the name of riches, is, essentially, power over man; in its simplest sense, the power of obtaining for our own advantage the labour of servant, tradesman, and artist; in wider sense, authority in directing large masses of the nation to various ends ... And this power of wealth of course is greater or less in direct proportion to the poverty of the men over whom it is exercised, and in inverse proportion to the number of persons who are as rich as ourselves, and who are ready to give the same price for an article of which the supply is limited. (Ruskin [1860] 1901: 43–4)

In other words – and history recounts this, although perhaps by its absence – in an ideal or communist world in which there is no inequality of income (and where by law and social compact it cannot be created) people would need other ideal motivations to work more than what is "owed" – in the language of Saint Paul (and Lenin) what is required are "new persons".

We find in Ruskin a profound and highly original critique of the nature of wealth:

> And therefore, the idea that directions can be given for the gaining of wealth, irrespectively of the consideration of its moral sources, or that any general and technical law of purchase and gain can be set down for national practice, is

perhaps the most insolently futile of all that ever beguiled
men through their vices.   (Ruskin [1860] 1901: 58)

Over 150 years later, these texts have lost none of their moral and
prophetic force. We created national accounting in the twentieth
century; we considered GDP an indicator of wealth and, indirectly
(then, not so indirectly), of well-being, and perhaps of happiness.
We will return to this theme later. Ruskin called us to reflect on the
nature of wealth, GDP, well-being and perhaps even to create other
indicators that fall when people are not doing well, and even hurt
themselves, while GDP rises. Ruskin knew all that; we must relearn
it. These are the themes of the civil economy, the themes of everyone's lives, and thus of ours as well.

4
Rents: Achille Loria

All for ourselves and nothing for other people, seems, in every
age of the world, the vile maxim of the masters of mankind.
  – Adam Smith, *The Theory of Moral Sentiments*, 1759

As we know from much historical evidence, economic science does
not always move forward with better responses to the same questions; it also changes some questions and forgets others. Questions
central to the classical era of economics (whether political or civil)
regarding income distribution, the nature of profit, the role of
rent were progressively abandoned by the neoclassical revolution
at the end of the nineteenth century. For example, what we today
call "income distribution" is quite different from its meaning in the
classical era, and we simply no longer talk about the origin of value
and profit.

The Italian political economist, Achille Loria (1857–1943), the
brother of the well-known mathematician Gino Loria, was a witness
to the great methodological revolution in economic science at the
end of the nineteenth century, and bitterly opposed its tendency
to abandon themes that he considered central even in the new
economics. Loria's scientific and human programme in particular

originated in response to this conflict, and in an era such as ours, of environmental and financial crisis, his criticisms of economic science are relevant and worth reconsidering today.

The centrality in Loria's work of the problem of rents – his central criticism of capitalism – make him an author that, to be understood correctly, should be considered within the civil economy tradition. Loria's scientific misfortune, in relation to his talent, was a consequence of his anachronism: he was born too late with respect to the classical paradigm and too early for today's. The first few decades of the twentieth century marked the eclipse of his themes by mainstream economics, not just on rents and income distribution, but also on land and his analysis of politics and institutions, themes which are now once again on the agenda in these crisis times. We find in Loria's work a theoretical and methodological apparatus that anticipated many of the topics at the centre of current economics, such as the economic analysis of law, institutions, political choices, as well as hints of theories of public goods, the commons, energy and land. In particular Loria should be present in every history of environmental economics, since his theory of rents is primarily a theory of land as a central resource of the socio-economic system. As he wrote in the introduction to his first work *La rendita fondiaria e la sua elisione naturale* (*Land Rent and Its Natural Elision*): "Land rent is not only the most important phenomenon of the entire social organism, it is its very summary" (Loria 1880: xiii).

In any case, within a few years, he went from being a beacon of a new economics to the symbol of an old, bizarre, syncretistic and undisciplined way of doing economic theory; by the time he was in his thirties he was already considered an economist in decline. His was a scientific (not academic) fate similar to what befell his friend and contemporary Maffeo Pantaleoni (1857–1924) after publishing his magnum opus, *Principi di economia pura* (*Principles of Pure Economics*) in 1889. Although Pantaleoni chose not to climb aboard the bandwagon of the new economic science, due to insufficient technical mathematical skills, nevertheless he continued to believe that there was but one true science, that of Pareto in particular. In contrast, Loria did not want to climb on board because he was convinced that the caravan would lead economic science in the wrong direction, off the right track indicated by the classics. This is also why Loria, particularly in the second phase of his life, was harshly judged by many scholars of his generation, among them Benedetto Croce, Antonio Gramsci (who coined the derogatory neologism "Lorianism"), Umberto Ricci, Antonio Labriola (perhaps his main adversary in Italy) and Friedrich Engels. In the preface to the third volume of *Capital* Engels wrote that:

Marx had hardly died, when Mr Achille Loria hastily published an article about him in the "Nuova Antologia" (April, 1883). He starts out with a biography of Marx full of disinformation, and follows it up with a critique of Marx's public, political and literary activity. He misrepresents the materialist conception of history and twists it with an assurance which indicates a great purpose.   (Marx [1894] 1909: 28)

Despite that, without outstanding students (or lacking that, a group of admirers) and with an army of bitter enemies and detractors (and very few allies and defenders in the Turin Laboratory, which Loria directed for thirty years), he continued to produce monumental works with the most prestigious publishers of his time, wrote an impressive number of articles, remained present in the most important journals of the leading countries in the world, wrote prefaces for books of young scholars who wanted to associate their works with him, and was a member of innumerable scientific societies. His life spanned from the young Alfred Marshall to the late John Maynard Keynes, and he attentively followed developments in the new marginalist economic theory; he knew it well enough to criticize it, as is clearly evident from his posthumous autobiography *Una crociera eccezionale* (*An Exceptional Journey*, 1947). Choosing not to embrace the new marginalist economics or the shift in the discipline to mathematics, which began in the last quarter of the nineteenth century, he saw these changes as not just an evolution of technique and method, but as abandoning the great classic themes, such as development, public happiness and above all income distribution, and refounding the science on subjectivity and hedonism. This was far from his sensibilities: "let us return to political economy. Unfortunately it has degenerated into a psychology created by those who are ignorant about psychology" (Loria 1947: 93).

To fully understand Loria's work and his intellectual figure we must connect him not only to Ricardo and the classical European economists but to the Italian civil tradition as well, including Genovesi and Verri, as well as Giandomenico Romagnosi and Carlo Cattaneo, and which continued after Loria with Piero Sraffa, Claudio Napoleoni, Paolo Sylos Labini, Giorgio Fuà and Giacomo Becattini. On the themes of income distribution, social class and a more territorial or local view of the economy they were the heirs of Loria – generally implicitly – more than of Pareto and Pantaleoni. Loria expressed an Italian tradition of economic science that Ferrara, Pareto and their followers never had or understood; that is why they wanted to keep their distance from it.

And yet Loria was an original economist with depth and worth re-evaluating in our era of financial capitalism. As nearly always happens, his ethical stature is revealed by the conclusion of his life. From 1919 until his death in 1943 (in Piedmont while hiding from the Nazis) he was a senator in the Kingdom of Italy and throughout that period he stayed well clear of fascism, never staining his career with serious moral crimes unlike Pantaleoni (who explicitly supported fascism and adopted its anti-Semite ideology).

Even though his criticism of capitalism matured in isolation and in parallel with the science of his time, which proceeded with different content and methods, because of its tenacity and coherence his thought remains important, with a strong, clear message and an interesting history to tell. Loria's work can still be mined today for very useful ideas and insights, not only to more deeply understand the decisive period in the birth of contemporary economics and the social sciences during the decades bridging the nineteenth and twentieth centuries, but also because they offer rich suggestions for understanding capitalism as we know it, or as we have known it so far.

Rents and land: two forgotten categories

Picking up and developing insights already present in his doctoral dissertation (the best ideas frequently come from the very young), Loria maintained that the principal and fundamental conflict of capitalism was not profits and salaries, but between *rentiers* and entrepreneurs:

> The real, basic schism in the two classes of wealth that traces an indelible furrow in all human affairs in the history of civilization, is that between the class of land owners and the class of capitalists; they have antithetical and opposing interests, and thus are in perennial conflict.   (Loria 1910: 211)

This thesis, which Loria had already laid out in the *Rendita fondiaria*, matured over the course of his work, finally becoming its dominant theme. His *Analisi della proprietà capitalista* (*An Analysis of Capitalist Property*, 1889) and *La costituzione economica* (*The Economic Constitution*, 1899) were two important stages in that process. Rent ("monopoly rent", as Loria called it) becomes the enemy of economic development and social production in a country, since it obstructs the actions of "capitalist-entrepreneurs" (Loria 1899: 79), that is, of productive capitalists (an important theme to which we will return). Unable to adequately invest their capital due to the dominant presence of rents, they are left holding what Loria called "excess systematic capital", which becomes de facto an unexpressed productive potential: "Landowners, either by deliberately holding back part of their land or by offering the rest under conditions that discourage the deployment of capital, make it impossible to productively use some fraction of total capital" (*ibid.*: 84ff.). And, if the rent is a universal monopoly rent (and not a Ricardian differential rent that is paid only on the most fertile land), the excess systematic capital "must therefore necessarily stagnate as excess capital". Loria then added a consideration that seems to have been written for today:

> This excess capital can eventually condemn a plot of land to non-productivity that would otherwise be productively employed, thus increasing the extent of abandoned land; but in any case, bringing competition to employed capital works forcefully to diminish the profit margin of that capital, to the exclusive advantage of monopoly rents.   (Loria 1899: 85)

Loria introduced the role of the state in this context, which by interventions to reform property structures, or by radically nationalizing land, could resolve the problem of rents at the source and unblock capitalist development, thus surpassing capitalism itself. However, he was aware that "with unyielding tenacity landowners resist all attempts to actualize such reformist measures" (*ibid.*: 80). This constant dynamic can be seen today as well, when those who own large financial rents react with every means available to them to oppose any tax proposal affecting them or any structural reform (such as the Tobin Tax or similar), which then remain, as did Loria's proposals, "in the gloomy limbo of social utopias". The historical evolution of capitalism and land rents led capitalists to become allies among themselves (along the lines of labour unions), as well as to ally themselves with landowners against the proletariat for survival. This too is quite current when we consider that the large multinational corporations are in the hands of investment funds.

Another matter of current interest is to extend his analysis of rents and development to the entire economy (not just the agricultural economy, to which many thought his system was limited), from the circulation of wealth to its redistribution: the dynamics of land rent are representative of the dynamics of the social organism, including the credit system. Loria gave considerable attention to the credit system; he came to define a land mortgage as an "economic parasite" because it serves no productive purpose and is thus an unproductive use of wealth, particularly in the many cases in which the mortgage interest exceeds the normal interest rate and the rate of return on invested capital: "How can the interest on a particular capital be greater than the profit it returns when employed under the direction of and together with the borrower's labour?" (Loria 1899: 591). The conclusion of his argument is that it leads to an inevitable economic depression: agricultural entrepreneurs cannot pay their creditors, leading to a structural crisis in the economy, with the added effect that "the depression hits the working class much worse than the banking class" (*ibid.*: 610).

Loria developed a highly critical position regarding rent-takers – and not just landowners – as is evident in the following passage from *La sintesi economica* (*An Economic Summary*), his final systematic work, in which the themes of his youth are even more clear and radical:

There is another distinction in the social classes that is shaped by the distinction between productive and unproductive capital: there are productive capitalists who are dedicated exclusively to industry, and unproductive capitalists, bankers who do not increase the wealth of society but rather speculate on securities, whose income is extracted from others' income. And that is not all. There are urban landowners who constitute an independent class that has its own exclusive, special interests; it favours urbanization, which concentrates the populace, resulting in an enormous increase in the price of developed land. There are country landowners who have diametrically opposed interests: they need to limit migration away from agriculture; they want to suppress industrial coercion, which urbanizes the entire populace, deprives the country of manual labour, and drives up salaries.

(Loria 1909: 211)

A different idea about society

His more structuralist vision of capitalism recurs throughout his main works, but particularly in *Le basi economiche della costituzione sociale* (*The Economic Bases of the Constitution of Society*, 1902). It is an imposing and ambitious text in which the author analyses capitalist society in the light of his theory of free land and social classes. In it he unleashed a veritable critique of society, its politics, law, morality and economy, that in certain ways anticipated by a century contemporary analyses by scholars of law, economics and political economy, and in general the economic approach to analysing religion and institutions; contemporary analyses may have a greater technical apparatus, but they rarely have the same depth of thought. The theme of the book is laid out in the first page:

Anyone who dispassionately observes human society as it unfolds before our eyes in all civil countries notices that it presents the strange phenomenon of an absolute, irrevocable schism between two rigorously distinct classes. One of them appropriates to itself enormous and increasing incomes without doing anything, and the other, far more numerous, works from the morning to the evening of its life in exchange for a meagre remuneration; the one lives without working, while the other works without living, or without living humanely. (Loria 1902: 1)

Loria's philosophy of history was based on the idea that the division into classes, and the oppression of one class by the other, originated and originates in the transition from what he called the "limit society" characterized by "free land" to capitalist society, in which land is no longer free and is appropriated by the dominant class. (He cited the American and Australian colonies, as well as the Tuscan Maremma region, as examples.)

When there is free land on which one can begin production by one's own labour, when a man without capital can, whenever he wants, appropriate an unoccupied plot of land, capitalist property is categorically impossible, since no worker will make himself available to work for a capitalist when he can freely appropriate a plot of land that has no price. In such conditions, each producer occupies for himself the plot of land that he can work with his labour (which we designate by the name *land unit*); at first he works it with his labour, and later with his labour and the capital he has accumulated. (Loria 1902: 1–2)

This theory of "free land", given here in its basic elements, is what made Loria's name known to the international economic community. It was also his misfortune as a theoretical economist, because it was too far from the new neoclassical sensibilities. Actually it is part of a complex and quite interesting theory critical of capitalism. *Il capitalismo e la scienza* (*Capitalism and Science*), published in 1901, is a small but important book because it marks the end of the "first phase" of Loria's thought. Loria wrote this book to respond to the many criticisms raised against his earlier works on land rents, free land and his theory of salary and income distribution. Actually, he had very few detractors; in Italy the most important was Pareto, whose public (but not private) silence was deafening. It is impressive to note the number of reviews, references and comments to Loria's works when he first burst onto the Italian and international economic scene in the 1880s. Indeed, his works were frequently reviewed and discussed in the United States, Germany and France, where they were translated.

Loria's principal source was Ricardo's theory of rent, whom he considered the first true economist and the one who systematized economic science. Loria integrated it with an elaborate population theory that, although of Malthusian origin, had important original elements. In his *La rendita fondiaria* (*Land rent*), Loria again placed the Ricardian theory of rent at the centre of his social analysis; after Marx land rent had lost its centrality with the reduction from a three factor capital–labour–land conflict to a two factor capitalist–labour conflict. However, Loria was convinced that the share of economic value (which he called "income") assigned to rents and its tendency to grow, were what characterized capitalism. This was in contrast to pre-capitalist societies in which rent was de facto truncated and redistributed to the different social classes in various ways. Growth in rents inexorably reduced the share of added value that went to companies, to industrial and productive capital, and thus to the development of the economy. The real conflict between entrepreneurs and workers, which drove down salaries, was a consequence of this more radical conflict between profits and rents. Loria maintained in Rousseauesqe-style – and he provided much historical evidence, still of great interest today – that the original condition of human society was characterized by common or "free land".

As Loria recounted it, in the Roman era, when forms of private property began to emerge, the important *ager publicus* ("public land") still existed:

In the medieval era, when individual property was prevalent and extensive, there was no lack of example of collective property such as servile communities made up of serfs who worked lands entrusted to them by the Lord ... But in general the phenomenon of collective property is disappearing by degrees from society ... We too accept this theory as true[1] of original collective property. (Loria 1910: 245)

A profound criticism of capitalism was hidden behind his theory of free land. In the *Corso completo di economia politica* (*A Complete Course in Political Economy*, 1910), he wrote:

The truth is that underneath the normal, healthy economic world that the classical school likes to depict, underneath crofters' farms and extensive estates, workshops and factories, in shadowy cellars a restless mob of forgers manipulates and traffics in others' wealth, fraudulently extracting very high gains from it. Ignored and neglected until now by

1. This refers to the theory of Émile de Laveleye that land property emerged historically as collective, attributed originally to the Commune, to the state, and generally to the collectivity (see Laveleye 1974).

the enthusiasts of the official science, this new science must publicly bring this degenerate and unwholesome world to the fore, disclosing its infamous ostentation and its iniquitous, shady laws. (Loria 1910: 303)

A "degenerate and unwholesome" world, which after a century mainstream economic science continues to ignore and neglect despite the evident damage it has provoked and continues to provoke.

Loria's insight and the battles he fought have today become decidedly crucial, when we observe the exponential increase in rents (in finance, by managers, by lobbies, and so forth), as well as the progressive return of salaries to subsistence levels following the constant increase in indirect levies and cuts to services and welfare. The abandonment of the theme of income redistribution and the destination of the surplus to the social classes, which was the central theme of classical economics, is due to the marginalist revolution and the individualistic ideology underlying it. By shifting attention from social class and income distribution to utility and individual choice, it has propagated the idea that every production factor receives a compensation proportional to its marginal productivity value, without anyone ever having explained how to measure the marginal productivity of managers or shareholders.

Returning to Loria's questions is important for anyone today who wants to continue a civil critique of capitalism. It is significant and can be read as a sign of the times that numerous important books on income distribution and the dizzying increase in inequality have been published in the past five years – one of the most recent being Thomas Piketty's *Capital in the Twenty-First Century* (2014). We close this chapter with the words of the philosopher Antonio Labriola (1843–1904), an intellectual adversary of Loria's, who however formulated one of the most honest judgements about him:

Loria, by culture, preparation and inclination, remains the most representative of all Italian economists of the last thirty years; someday when a diligent scholar wants to glean the best material from the Analysis, the Modern Economic Constitution and the Summary, Achille Loria will appear in a new light in the history of Italian thought of recent years.

(Labriola 1912: xiii)

5

The "Catholic" spirit of capitalism:
Amintore Fanfani

One can behold in capitalism a religion.
— Walter Benjamin, "Capitalism as Religion", 1921

The historian Amintore Fanfani's work has important things to say about the nature of our form of capitalism, and specifically about Italian and European capitalism. In a work, like this, on the classics and the ideas of the civil economy, it is worth bringing Fanfani's ideas back into the collective memory, even if briefly.

The Protestant Reformation left a profound mark on modern culture, and it should not be surprising that the spirit of modernity and the spirit of the Reformation are tightly interwoven. There was a period of thought from the end of the nineteenth century until the 1930s in which there was great interest in the historical causes and roots of modernity, its relationship to the Reformation, and the reactions against it (we will summarily call this the Catholic Counter-Reformation, knowing that the expression was and is ambiguous). Giuseppe Toniolo, Werner Sombart, Lujo Brentano, Gino Luzzatto, Amintore Fanfani and Max Weber were historians and social scientists who made the thought and work of Martin Luther and the other sixteenth-century reformers (Calvin in particular) the axis around which they reconstructed the coordinates of modernity. They gave special attention to the birth of capitalism, which they considered an ethos, or "spirit" of modernity, thus something far more general and pervasive than just the economics (production, savings, circulation and consumption) of European and Western societies. Placing the accent on "spirit" – a very common expression in the modern social sciences from Montesquieu to Weber – meant emphasizing that capitalism was not just material in nature, thus affirming that entrepreneurs, bankers, consumers and other protagonists see the market and companies as much more than the supply and demand of goods mediated by money. This concept was also present in Marx, and in the twentieth century it was developed by such thinkers as Ernst Block and Walter Benjamin (as well as by Weber). If we do not grasp the "religious", symbolic and "spiritual" nature of capitalism, it is difficult to understand the *sola fide* that is the basis for speculative finance, and that has lost all ties with the *res* (the real side of the economic problem).

The historical analysis of the "spirit of capitalism" has been in a long eclipse from the 1930s to today (see Zamagni 2010). Recently, however, there has been a renewed interest on the part of historians and social scientists in the origins of capitalism and its spirit. Among these are the French authors Eve Chiapello and Luc Boltansky, who called their important work *The New Spirit of Capitalism* (2007). The sociologist Mauro Magatti is working on this theme in Italy, continuing the tradition of the Catholic University of Milan, which with Fanfani and his school (Gino Barbieri, for example) made significant contributions to these themes between the two world wars, emphasizing the "Catholic spirit" of capitalism. For Chiapello and Boltansky, what characterizes the modern spirit of capitalism is its capacity to "recycle" and incorporate the major criticisms made of it during its history (and primarily those made recently), and then turn them into the main factors of change and innovation. Thus the "social" criticisms (socialist, communist, cooperativist, labour and environmental), rather than provoking its collapse, as they might have done, became its cornerstones at the end of the twentieth century, giving life to a new capitalism, a new "spirit". This is true in companies as well, primarily in large multinational firms, in which we see the development of social balances and social businesses, with attention to worker well-being, equal opportunities, and even the recent concepts of corporate "symbolic" or "spiritual" capital. In parallel with the inclusion and transformation of social criticism, this capitalism has also internalized aesthetic criticisms, giving life to a new season of creativity. The main giants of the new economy, such as Google and Apple, have made "creatives" their new entre- preneurs and lead players. In chameleon-like fashion, capitalism is transforming itself, finding sustenance in whatever it finds along the way. For Chiapello and Boltansky, this capacity to change and incor- porate criticism is the new spirit of capitalism, which preserves very little of its old Calvinist origins.

Amintore Fanfani (1908–99) was among the scholars who, on an international scale, dug most deeply into the relationship between Christianity, the Reformation, the Counter-Reformation and economics; his work, like others in this book, awaits rediscovery today. Fanfani's starting point was the contrast between the medi- eval era and Renaissance humanism. In the Middle Ages – and here he echoed some of Jacques Maritain's themes in *Integral Humanism* (1936) – the centre was God, but with humanism, humanity became the centre, with individualism its usual characteristic, which was expressed in all spheres of human endeavour, from economics to art. In the Middle Ages economic ethics were dominated by the idea of justice and by the principle of being content with one's status. Thus seeking and accumulating "excessive" wealth was condemned (primarily by Aquinas). Each should seek wealth "adequate" to one's needs, without ambitiously seeking an excess; accepting one's lot was what upheld the social order organized into strata, classes and groups.

Fanfani, however, after showing the conflict between Catholic and capitalist ethics, posed a question that today still occupies scholars (e.g. see B. S. Gregory 2012). In 1934 Fanfani wrote: "if Catholicism has fought the capitalist spirit, then and always, why did it manifest itself in the Catholic era?" His response was that the pre-Reformation spirit of capitalism emerged from several "deviations" that were due to a new set of realities during the fifteenth and sixteenth centuries: international commerce and merchants' actions that were beyond local control; the expulsion of Jews from the south to the north of Europe; the displacement of commerce from the Mediterranean to the Atlantic. For Fanfani, the Protestant spirit is just one of these new realities. Indeed, in an essay written as a mature historian, *Capitalism, Collectivity and Participation*, we read: "The weakening of influence of the social conception proposed and supported by medieval Catholicism is the circumstance which explains the manifestation and growth of the capitalistic spirit in a Catholic world" (Fanfani [1976] 2002). Thus, in Fanfani's judgement the Reformation reinforced, but did not initiate, the deviation from the Gospel message that had already begun to manifest itself in the Catholic milieu.

The central point of Fanfani's critique is that the real conflict that led to the Reformation was not theological, but rather a conflict between two civilizations: the Germanic world, and Italian and Latin humanism. Fanfani wrote: "When the Germanic world came into contact with the Latin world, which had been refined by Renaissance manners, it withdrew in horror. Luther harshly judged the nature of the renewal and reacted" (Fanfani 1968: 508). Indeed, for the Italian humanists, the world appeared to be a garden of delights, populated by inhabitants preoccupied with improving hospitality, and deepening the powerful gifts of ingenuity in imagining new juxtapositions and combinations. In the words of the humanist Coluccio Salutati, the happy creatures did not deny the initial creative intervention of a beneficent God, but they reasoned "as if there were no God". Humanity appeared at the centre of society. [Thus] the Reformation, which formally began and took strength from him [Luther], was first of all a protest, then a restoration. ... in the eyes of his initial followers the world in which humanity dominated was heretical, the society in which neighbours, goods, time, ingenuity, and worship were about making the enjoyment of life easier for the individual.

(Fanfani 1968: 508)

This theme was not dissimilar to Weber's: "And what the reformers complained of in those areas of high economic development was not too much supervision of life on the part of the Church, but too little" (Weber 2008: 5).

This statement seems bizarre to us (because we have forgotten the importance of the religious element in life), but if purged of a certain apologetic vein in defence of the Catholic world and a thinly veiled anti-Protestantism of that time, it retains a certain heuristic capacity, primarily for a discourse on capitalism. Luther's protest – and Calvin's even more so – was against Civic Humanism and the Renaissance, as well as against the theological deviations (such as indulgences) and the clergy's way of life. Fanfani wrote:

The Latin world reacted against the Protestant criticisms, but the reaction was predominantly ecclesiastical. The Counter-Reformation, while sharing early Protestantism's criticisms of humanistic and Renaissance ideals, distinguished these from its own; it acted such that people would make use of the arts and letters that Civic Humanism and the Renaissance had rediscovered and perfected in order to lead a life enlightened by Christian ideals.   (Fanfani 1968: 509)

So for Fanfani "Humanism-Renaissance and Protestantism unfolded along the same track, in that they were moments of the same revelation that humanity did to itself: the 'naturalistic' revelation" (*ibid.*).

At this point Fanfani's discourse opens onto a highly relevant theme: Humanism–Renaissance and the Protestant Reformation were two reforms of the medieval spirit, two different transitions from "voluntarist" doctrines (that is, that humans are diseased and must be oriented towards the good by institutions, and thus by the hierarchy) to "naturalist" doctrines (individual interests are good). Thus the Counter-Reformation sought to restore the Middle Ages, while the Protestant Reformation more forcefully continued the work of Humanism and the Renaissance. Hence the distinction between

the northern countries, in which Reformation individualism was oriented towards production and the creation of wealth, and Catholic countries (also due to the weight of classic Roman culture), in which the Counter-Reformation blocked that subjectivist revolution and returned the world to medieval ethics – ending up however accomplishing nothing except encouraging conspicuous, positional consumption and discouraging corporate economic activity and work.
(Fanfani 1968: 512)

The Catholic Church reacted against the values of the Reformation by questioning the values of Humanism and the Renaissance against which the Reformation had inveighed, and in so doing ended up obstructing the process of European humanism, which was constructing a market economy based on liberty. That is why the northern cities of Europe gave life to capitalism, while the Latin cities saw a restoration of anti-modern values, especially rents and consumption. In other words, according to Fanfani, the Reformation and the consequent Counter-Reformation blocked the humanist process that began in the Middle Ages and gave rise to Civic Humanism and a capitalism that was at once personalistic and communal, a capitalism capable of melding individual liberty and the common good, with a fundamental role played by the great medieval charisms, theologians, citizens' institutions, and their liberty within the city walls. From one aspect Protestantism criticized humanist and Renaissance customs, and it was much less conspicuous in the trappings of wealth than the Catholic Church of that time. However, by eliminating the church's mediation and control in citizens' lives, it ended up creating a climate of unmediated liberty for people, in which capitalism developed in its own way (although without the social dimension, except for philanthropy and restorative ethics) – in the market economy of the fourteenth through to the seventeenth centuries.

The Reformation is a noteworthy case of unintended consequences, although not the only one in modernity. Luther and the other proponents of the Reformation (except Calvin) were hostile to economic questions, not knowing how market institutions operated. Theirs was an impassioned fight against the widespread practice in the Catholic Church of corruption and commerce in indulgences. The Reformation did not pertain, except indirectly, to the ethical sphere. It was focused instead on theology and religious life. And yet, preoccupied as he was with protecting religion from the influence of market forces, by affixing his Ninety-Five Theses to the Wittenberg cathedral door, Luther wrote – according to some interpreters of Weber's work – a capitalist manifesto. Is there any truth to that? We do not think so. In the first place, contrary to the assertions of no small number of interpreters, Weber never maintained that capitalism originated in the Reformation. Weber in fact wrote:

> We have no intention whatever of maintaining such a foolish and doctrinaire thesis as that the spirit of capitalism (in the provisional sense of the term explained above) could only have arisen as the result of certain effects of the Reformation, or even that capitalism as an economic system is a creation of the Reformation. (Weber 2008: 91)

According to Weber, it is not so much capitalism per se as it is *modern* capitalism that requires an explanation of its origins, or better yet, of its rapid spread in the northern European countries. Note that in contrast to Luther, whose knowledge of economic problems was rather limited and whose hostility to capitalist practices was well known, Calvin was fully aware of financial practices and their economic and social implications in Geneva, where he lived. One can support the view that, although bourgeois values such as frugality, perseverance, dedication to one's work and so forth all received explicit recognition in Calvin's theology, modern capitalism (in Weber's sense) is more a collateral result than the expected outcome of that religious perspective – a perspective in which salvation is something individual rather than communal.

While for Catholic theology sin is destructive of the unity of the human race, for Protestant theology sin is the rupture of the individual bond that unites one to God; this is how salvation becomes an eminently individual fact. The practical consequence of such a change in perspective was that Catholic social works were eliminated in countries touched by the Reformation; that is to say, one of the highest expressions of the centrality of the common good was abandoned. That in turn had the effect of transferring a sizeable amount of resources from social to economic use, thus favouring the process of capital accumulation. To put it another way, the Reformation not only influenced the demand side – as most hold – by altering people's dispositions and preferences towards a higher propensity for work and saving, but the supply side as well, resulting in a substantial reduction in the cost of services and religious practices. Eliminating the hierarchy, indulgences, pilgrimages and other religious rites, building modest churches, and so forth, all had the effect of freeing up scarce resources (labour and capital) and channelling them towards economically productive uses.

The large scale anti-feudal movement during the eighteenth century in southern Europe, or the providential vision of the market and commerce (one need only consider Genovesi or Dragonetti in Catholic Enlightenment Naples in the second half of the eighteenth century) cannot be understood apart from a Catholic Europe that, after the sixteenth century, did not find its way back to a "civil" market for two or three centuries and that, in place of the civil and commercial virtues of Siena, Florence, Venice and Marseilles, had established rural virtues and virtues in consumption. Then, as now, in a Europe seeking a way towards the market and civil society, there was a need for a civil economy.

Voluntarism and naturalism

An important key to understanding the whole of Fanfani's discourse is the distinction between *voluntarist* and *naturalist* doctrines.[1] The

---

1. The naturalist/voluntarist metaethical debate on the origins of morality is deeply rooted in the Middle Ages. In the naturalist view, people are capable of knowing and following moral principles (although they are capable of failing to do so). In the voluntarist view, morality is determined by what God commands, or what his delegated earthly governing agents command through the political process.

medieval world, as well as the Greco-Roman world, was voluntaristic, thus politics was primary. The modern world proclaims naturalism, in which the primacy shifts to the economy, with no further need for mediation:

> The politician is finally deposed. He is no longer the regulator of human life ... The discovery of the immanence of the rational order has rendered his busybody ways superfluous, rather, it considered him as harmful. His mission is to live at the margins of the economy, which concedes him the crumbs it deems less convenient. The relationship between the economy and politics, as they were established by modern voluntarists, is overturned. Even politics is exonerated of its function of maintaining the economy on a moral level. The free contest of selfish actors also brings about the enormous effect of creating not only the most economic order, but the best and most just order as well.   (Fanfani 1942: 176)

Classic voluntarism, particularly in its medieval and proto-modern version, began with the assumption that the human being was afflicted with selfishness *but remained a social animal capable of having relationships*. Its biblical root, grafted onto that of the Greeks, had recognized and affirmed the social nature of the person (as seen in the Scholastics – in Aquinas in particular – and the Franciscans), as well as the need for institutions and social norms to keep this fragile social nature from becoming "afflicted".[2] In particular, that anthropology – and especially Christian anthropology – saw the human being as an ambivalent reality, capable of virtue and vice together.

---

2. Aristotle's views on wealth, or chrematistics, is almost unaltered in Aquinas and throughout the Middle Ages.

Institutions played a fundamental role because they allowed the virtuous social animal to express itself, while checking and limiting the "vicious" side. Virtue is natural and co-essential in human beings. Beginning with the Greeks, the basic message of virtue ethics is that of an anthropological realism: the person is at once virtuous and vicious, *agape* and selfish. It is thus necessary to develop education, schools, rewards and institutions that reinforce virtue. This is what voluntarism was about: the common good must be institutionally constructed, rather than considered as emerging from vices. A key element in this humanism is the mediation of the institutions, which remained "communal" and relational (not automatic or anonymous). Scepticism regarding contractualist theories originates in the idea that the human being is social by nature and does not become sociable by a social contract.[3]

The Reformation was much more than a religious event: it was an epochal turning point. Protestant anthropology, due to its Augustinian pessimism (present and exacerbated in Luther and Calvin), no longer believed that mankind is capable of positive reciprocity, at least in the public and economic spheres. It thus avoids direct cooperation, and the great theme of the common good emerges from the interplay of interests because we cannot expect anything more from human nature. Truly, according to Protestant theology, humans live in society, but only because they are driven there by necessity and convenience, not because it follows from their sociable natures, as Aristotle taught. Life in community is seen as a experienced fact of the human condition, and it is lived out as an inescapable restraint. The human person is basically a rational,

---

3. As has been noted, the social contract originates from a pessimistic anthropology; it was explicit in Hobbes and present as well in Rousseau, although he held that in a stage in the distant past humanity was sociable, which was ruined by civilization.

selfish entity that is interested in maximizing her objective function, subject to restraints indicated by a theologically grounded ethics.

Such a view excludes that reciprocity – and thus gratuitousness[4] – is an essential dimension of a human person, which the anthropology underlying the theological line through Augustine, Aquinas and early Scholasticism had forcefully maintained. The French, Scottish and Italian Enlightenments vehemently reacted against this illiberal and "a-civil" view, not against humanism's reciprocity. Reciprocity was taken up by the French Revolution in the category of fraternity – even though, as is known, it was later abandoned and even opposed. The paradigm of instrumental rationality, or rational choice, that is at the heart of modern capitalism thus found favourable ground for cultivation in Protestant spirituality.

In other words, as Latouche showed in *La sfida di Minerva* (*Minerva's Challenge*; 2000), the Reformation broke the bond that had held the two dimensions of reason together: the "older son" of the goddess Minerva, *Phrónesis* (wisdom, reasonableness) and the "younger son", *Lógos epistemonikós* (geometrical reason). The result was that Minerva's two "spiritual sons" separated: "Protestant rationality" became identified with *Lógos*, and "Mediterranean reason" with *Phrónesis*.

---

4. Gratuitousness, a pivotal concept in the authors' thought, should be understood in the sense of a free and open gift, or offering, in a larger setting of reciprocal exchanges between peers. Significantly, gratuitousness is not motivated by altruism, but by the intention of establishing an interpersonal relation. In such an exchange, in offering something to another I do so freely, gratuitously, without obligating the recipient to some form of return. In such direct interactions I will eventually be hurt by someone who betrays my offer, my gift, but if I can respond in gratuitousness, I can model and foster reciprocity in society. Reciprocity depends on gratuitousness; reciprocity may not develop unless someone takes the risk of being hurt by making a gratuitous gesture. It differs from the neoclassical economic view that focuses on the goods or services exchanged, for the authors the relationship with the other is the primary good; above all, that relationship must be preserved to live our lives to the fullest. (*Trans.*)

In the voluntarist vision, economic order is not spontaneous. In this regard Fanfani wrote:

There are three possible conceptions of the spontaneity (or lack thereof) of the economic order: either one believes that the rational and most beneficial economic order is immanent; or that the rational and beneficial economic system does not spontaneously actualize but can be realized without insurmountable obstacles if humanity bows to human reason; or finally that it does not spontaneously actualize but can be realized if humanity bows to human reason, although encountering obstacles that sometimes can, and sometimes cannot, be overcome ... Economic doctrines based on the first conception [spontaneous order], believing in the existence of an immanent rational economic order and ... believing useless any attempt to modify the economic order that actualizes according to natural laws, will reduce all possible *norms* to just one: let the natural laws operate freely. ... The proposed name for these doctrines is "naturalistic", and the movement of ideas represented by them is called "economic naturalism" ... Economic doctrines based on the second conception of economic order, believing in the non-existence of an immanent rational and beneficial order ... [and] believing instead in the necessity of rationalizing economic life according to the principles of right reason and the ideals indicated by them when determining presuppositions, will enumerate very many *norms* that are capable of guiding humanity towards the realization of a considered rational economic order, the result of the will in the service of reason. Due to the trust in the human will, evident in these doctrines, as the means for realizing the ideals suggested by reason, the proposed name for these doctrines is *voluntaristic* and *economic voluntarism*.

(Fanfani 1942: 34)

Due to its "Catholic" cultural roots, the civil economy, and more generally the European and Italian economic and political traditions, have always taken a voluntaristic approach (consider the mixed economy, for example, and the great weight of the state in the economy) until recent times, when conformist mainstream thought originating in naturalism has become dominant. The voluntaristic approach requires economic behaviours to be tempered by society to ensure growth, and thus the common good, for everyone (not just the most talented or those that have a competitive head start). The theories of just price, salaries, money and usury as stated by Aquinas, Nicola d'Oresme, Bernardino da Siena, Giovanni Botero, Antonino da Firenze and many others are part of this voluntarist tradition, including the Franciscans (whom a certain "naturalistic" reading of the history of economics tends to place in this camp).

It is not so much that the medieval theories did not grasp the nature of the market as a positive sum game (this too is found in other authors), nor that they did not understand the incentivizing nature of interests and profits; what is in play here is a vision of society and humanity in which the good does not emerge from selfishness, but from the virtues. Genovesi's civil economy is obviously in the voluntarist tradition as well. Fanfani writes:

> The Italian abbot Antonio Genovesi was the leading figure of all, who in 1754 had the fortune to be the first to occupy a university chair in economics in Naples, and who systematically organized the entire modern voluntaristic doctrine in a fully developed form in the *Lezioni di economica civile* ... Genovesi wrote in the preface to the Italian translation of John Cary's *Essay on the State of England*, "Nature gives people instincts, but the government must give form and skill." (Fanfani 1942: 165–7)

The eclipse of virtues

A key to understanding Fanfani's discourse on the voluntarism/ naturalism distinction – which is being taken up today by scholars such as Tullio Gregory as a truly central and fundamental point for understanding our civil and economic culture – is his discussion of virtue ethics and how it was interpreted by the Reformation and Catholicism.[5]

Until modernity, the Middle Ages and humanism had placed virtue ethics – a combination of Aristotelian, Stoic and Christian ethics synthesized primarily by Aquinas – at the centre of individual and social life. Despite sin and vices, human beings are capable of virtue (actions done because they are good in themselves) and they are not "afflicted" to the point of losing either their natural social capacity, or *agape* (as recorded in Genesis, Adam was not eradicated by Cain and Lameck). With the Reformation, and above all with Luther, the Augustinian anthropology that until then had been one core principle of Christian humanism, but neither the only nor the main one, was exacerbated and became dominant, and with it the idea that humanity was so afflicted with selfishness as to make it incapable of virtue, at least in the city of man – that is, in the city of politics and economics. It was then that the idea began to be asserted in Protestant countries that interest and utility were the real motives of human action (consider Hobbes, Mandeville and Smith); these were the only solid base on which to build social theories that could explain the "person as he is", rather than the imaginary people of Aristotelian and Thomist philosophy.

---

5. Fanfani returned to this distinction in 1991 in his final unpublished work, *Tre rivoluzioni industriali, due guerre mondiali, ed ora?* (*Three Industrial Revolutions, Two World Wars, and Now?*), which is now available in *Dall'Eden alla Terza guerra mondiale* (Fanfani [1991] 2014).

Tullio Gregory has written in this regard that: "In their [the reformers'] view, even after baptism people, without God, could only sin, and were not capable of doing anything for their own salvation" (T. Gregory 2013: 236). It is thus not surprising that in his *Open Letter to the Christian Nobility of the German Nation* Luther inveighed against Aristotle, defined as a "blind, heathen master ... damned, conceited, rascally heathen" (Luther [1520] 1915: 146). He described Aristotle's book on ethics as "the worst of all books. It flatly opposes divine grace and all Christian virtues" (*ibid.*: 147) and proposed a radical reform of the universities, where such pagan teachings should be banned. In criticizing Aristotle, Luther criticized and refuted Albert the Great, Aquinas, Peter Lombard and Scholasticism, which remained increasingly outside modern Protestant Europe (at least the Lutheran and Calvinist areas). Thus virtue ethics ended up being considered a legacy of medieval *Christianitas* and associated with Counter-Reformation Catholic Europe, and the great centres of modern political and economic theory that remained almost wholly Protestant in culture were far removed from its influence.

In this context we can better understand a central aspect of the civil economy tradition: in contrast to the political economy tradition, it remained anchored to virtue ethics, convinced that there were two primitive "forces" (in Genovesi's words), one egoistic, the other prosocial. The latter force and its "virtuous" tendency were never eradicated by sin and needed appropriate "rewards" to reinforce it otherwise it would atrophy (see Bruni & Zamagni 2014).

After a couple of centuries the ethics of our form of capitalism, which insists on a reductionistic and pessimistic anthropology operating solely at the level of individual interests and "sad passions" (in Spinoza's sense), is indeed producing sad economic agents that have atrophied in their capacity for virtue, and so unable to follow an ethic of duty and honour; our relational, environmental and political anthropology is impoverished with a consequent diminution of the joy of living, to which we can all attest.

Part II

Ideas

6

Why GDP is not enough

O human race, born to fly upward, wherefore at a little wind
dost thou so fall?
                                    – Dante, *Purgatorio*, Canto XII

The themes of well-being, approval, public happiness and a good
social life have been and are at the centre of the civil economy tradition, alongside the relationship between the well-being of nations,
of citizens and indicators such as GDP. In recent years, informed
by significant segments of civil society, debate has grown significantly on the necessity of surpassing GDP or of adding other indicators that report other dimensions of well-being. Some scholars
(such as Amartya Sen, Jean-Paul Fitoussi and Joseph Stiglitz) and
politicians are considering new measuring techniques of subjective happiness as well-being indicators that can work alongside, or
replace, GDP and other objective indicators. France, followed by
the United Kingdom, and now Italy as well, have initiated projects
aiming to directly measure their citizen's subjective well-being. This
is based on the hypothesis, supported by ample empirical evidence,
that in a postmodern world objective indicators are no longer sufficient to express how well people live, which increasingly depends

on non-monetary factors such as the quality of the natural environment, the availability of relational goods, and so forth.

However, the scenario that is taking shape is similar to what we might see with a football match. At the end of the game the different statistics appear on the screen: the percentage of possession by each team, fouls committed and suffered, the number of corner kicks, and so forth. However, at the top of the statistics, the number of goals dominates the rest; it is the only statistic that really counts, and which no other statistic listed can remotely modify. Indicators like the Human Development Index (HDI), the ecological impact, in Italy the Benessere Equo e Sostenibile (BES) – "Fair and Sustainable Well-being" – and others all resemble ball possession and corner kicks, which are ancillary to the number of goals scored (or GDP).

Another analogy, one closer to what we will soon need to implement in modern economies, comes from the great multi-stage cycling tours. In the Tour de France, there is a yellow jersey for the overall leader; there are also other jerseys that have their own prestige, emphasizing and rewarding other dimensions of excellence among the cyclists: the polka dot jersey for the best climber, the green sprinter's jersey, and the white jersey for the fastest young cyclist. There are cyclists who compete just for these other jerseys and in Paris every jersey is rewarded and applauded. A country's well-being indicators should follow a similar logic to that of the multi-stage tours: more jerseys, more classifications, and more rewards, since human excellence is multidimensional. There should be one difference, however: GDP should not represent the yellow jersey, but rather that should go to an index of well-being or public happiness. GDP should be the sprinter's jersey, since that best expresses a society's dimensions of efficiency, growth, and so forth.

The Italian tradition of social well-being

The research of the Italian economist Giorgio Fuà (1919–2000) centred around measuring well-being, GDP and happiness long before criticism of GDP and the new indicators burst on the scene. His work was fully in line with the civil economy. The same can be said about the French economist François Perroux (1903–87), who was among the first to speak out on the limits of GDP: "The price of living comes from things without price. Giving of what one has and what one is within the sphere of the gratuitousness act, a person attains her most incontestable dignity."

It is true that the theme of well-being (and not just riches) is present in the Scottish tradition of Adam Smith. This is evident from the title itself of the *Wealth of Nations*, rather than the *Riches of Nations*; "wealth", in contrast to "riches", refers back to *weal*, to *well-being*. That nexus is much stronger and more central in the civil economy.

The theme of public happiness was at the centre of the works of many Italian authors, including Ludovico Antonio Muratori, Giuseppe Palmieri, Isidoro Bianchi, Pietro Verri and many other authors of the eighteenth century. Paolo Mattia Doria began his work *Della vita civile* (*On Civil Life*) in 1710; it was an important source for Genovesi's thought and that of the Neapolitan school. It affirmed a clear relationship between civil life and public happiness, a union that produced the expression *civil economy* a few years later. "Without doubt, the primary object of our desires is human happiness" (Doria 1852: 1). We find happiness in the titles of various works by economists in the Kingdom of Naples of the period: Giuseppe Palmieri's *Riflessioni sulla pubblica felicità* (*Reflections on Public Happiness*), Ludovico Muratori's *Della pubblica felicità* and Pietro Verri's *Meditazioni sulla felicità* (*Meditations on Happiness*, 1763). The latter emphasized that: "the discourse *on happiness* has as its object a very common argument, about which very many have written" (Verri [1763] 1963: 3). There is a passage from Genovesi that is central to understanding this aspect of the idea of happiness:

> Work for your own interest. No one could work for other than his own happiness; he would be less than a man. But, do not desire to cause misery to others; if you can, and when you can, studiously try to make others happy. The more you work for your own interest, so much the more – as long as you are not crazy – must you be virtuous. It is a law of the universe that we cannot make ourselves happy without making others happy.
> (Genovesi 1963: 449)

The paradox here is in stating that happiness comes from making others happy, which is a theme with an Aristotelian and an even more Thomist flavour. For this tradition happiness has a paradoxical nature, precisely because it is fundamentally relational: one cannot live a "good life" unless it is with and thanks to others (making "others happy"). But for just this reason we do not have full control over happiness. A human being needs reciprocity to become herself, but for that she must make the leap to gratuitousness, which may not be reciprocated (herein lies a deadly risk, as Plato and other Greek philosophers warned.) In any case, without gratuitousness genuine reciprocity – and with it society – does not develop.[1]

The adjective "public" that normally precedes the word "happiness" is particularly meaningful, since it expresses the structurally social nature of happiness: *either it is public or it is not.* Even though the economists in the Kingdom of Naples, and in a certain

---

1. For a much fuller discussion on the themes of gratuitousness, happiness, and the risk of relational wounds in a larger economic setting see Bruni (2012).

measure the entire Italian tradition, attributed to public happiness a centrality that we can rightly consider as the principal characteristic of the classic Italian school of economics, that does not at all mean that the theme was a prerogative of Italy alone – although it should be recognized as having certain Latin, Catholic and communal origins. Distinct from the individual right to the pursuit of happiness, which is more typical of a Calvinist, individualist, North American culture, public happiness can be considered – and with reason – a fourth component of the reform programme of modernity, along with "liberty, fraternity, equality". Genovesi and the civil economy made a foundational contribution to this project, a project to fulfil in modernity.

There is the idea in the Anglo-American tradition that directly concerning oneself with riches is a means of concerning oneself, although indirectly, with well-being or happiness. In a world that was fighting for subsistence and that suffered an endemic lack of primary goods and resources, these ideas had some plausibility. At the same time, the Latin tradition, by placing public happiness directly at the centre of its thought as a specific and explicit goal, chose to concern itself with aspects on which the well-being of peoples and persons depend, such as social relationships, care for the good, and trust; these were all themes that Genovesi and other civil economists placed at the centre of their economic thought. Hence the adjective "civil" rather than "political", as it places emphasis on the interpersonal dimension ("civil" derives from the Roman *civitas*, while "political" derives from the Greek *polis*).

A few years after Adam Smith the Anglo-Saxon tradition found its new foundational philosophy in Bentham's utilitarianism and hedonism, thus partly breaking with Smith and the Scottish tradition of "moral sense". At the same time, the Latin and Catholic public happiness tradition inherited – although in deep dialogue with the modern philosophies of Descartes, Locke and even Rousseau and

Montesquieu – an Aristotelian and Thomist vision of happiness that had two essential guidelines: the fundamentally social or communal dimension of well-being (the common good) and the close relationship between public happiness and the cultivation of the virtues. The title of a book by the nineteenth-century Neapolitan economist Ludovico Bianchini, *La scienza del ben-vivere sociale* (*The Science of Social Well-being*), encapsulates well the civil economy project of the classic Italian tradition.

Public happiness exhibits a deep bond with civil fraternity; for our lives to be good, we have an extreme need for bonds and belonging, while accepting their ambivalence. If we live in a society that is no longer fraternal, but immunized and immunizing, civil life does not flourish, and happiness is not attained, or at least not fully. Moreover, happiness and fraternity are profoundly relational experiences, thus fragile and vulnerable, but both are essential for a good life. While Italians were reflecting on happiness, during those same years in France a new process was begun that led to the creation of GDP as the measure of economic well-being of a nation.

GDP says many things, but it says nothing about the well-being, quality of life, democracy, rights or freedoms of a nation. We know that, but every so often it is good to remind ourselves of it – particularly when we hear certain types of news. GDP indicates the production value of goods and services of a country in a given year, nothing more. At one time, in a simpler world, it was also an indicator of the number of job positions created and, therefore, perhaps of well-being; in a society that was emerging from indigence, increasing goods and services also increased families' well-being. Today it indicates increasingly less, and increasingly badly. The word "goods", that is, good things, has lost all contact with what we call economic goods. What good is there in pornography or prostitution? What good is there in games of chance and the legions of "scratch and win" tickets that are increasingly impoverishing our most fragile citizens? Nothing, but together they increase GDP: the more people ruin themselves playing slot machines, the more job positions there are, the more tax revenue increases (by too little) and GDP is greater. Even more serious from an ethical point of view is that part of these wrongful profits end up financing non-profit organizations and activities, which may well take care of the victims of these addictions. One may object and say this is how capitalism works, but it is no less sad for all that; those who love truth and justice should act to change it.

All this indicates just how little GDP says about the economic and civil health of a country. If, theoretically, Italy were to finally begin showing a positive GDP, thanks to an increase in games of chance, or the use of pornography, or arms sales, or prostitution, would we have good reason to celebrate? Someone might respond that the number of jobs would increase. But today, just as yesterday, not all jobs are good. What is the ethical and human cost of a woman who works in the porn industry in order to survive? Or of someone who works in a video lottery establishment where he witnesses the real tragedy of one who ruins herself to "play"? Or of someone who produces anti-personnel mines? There are awful jobs, and an authentic civilization is one that reduces wrongful jobs and increases beneficial ones. With the abolition of slavery in Europe and America hundreds of thousands of jobs were lost (think of the number of ships and ports that worked in this vile trade until the nineteenth century), but within a few decades industrial and tech-nological revolutions had come about precisely because slavery had ceased. True democracy – not just the market – is a "creative destruction" in which activities that are wrongful and harmful to persons cease, in order to create better ones that replace them.

The idea that economic well-being is but one part, although an important part, of an integral human well-being has always been alive within the civil economy tradition. For example, at the height of his academic career in 1993, Fuà wrote a small book called *Crescita economica: L'insidia delle cifre* (*Economic Growth: The Snare in the Numbers*) in which he argued, among others, a central theme: that GDP is no longer sufficient to measure the well-being of a nation, particularly in the more advanced stages of growth when an economy transitions from hard goods to immaterial goods, such as services, and intangible values. There is nothing new or original to this point, particularly within the Italian tradition. It is an argument that has been made since at least the 1950s by environmental economists, like Nicholas Georgescu-Roegen, and by writers critical of the capitalist model, such as John Kenneth Galbraith, or Tibor Scitovsky and is today emphasized anew, without either great cultural or technical innovations, by the various government commissions that study subjective well-being. In Fuà, an economist fully in line with the Italian tradition, we find, however, a stronger and more original reflection on the limits of GDP:

> in periods of great economic changes, and primarily in the service industry, GDP says little: we are not justified in celebrating or becoming alarmed because the speed of annual GDP growth is a half percentage point above or below what we expected, or with respect to what happened in the past or to what is happening in other countries.   (Fuà 1993: 106)

Fuà reminded us that it is very complicated, if not erroneous, to count services offered by the public sector in GDP, partly since, in his (and our) view, it is very difficult to add the value of services to that of goods. Furthermore, since this component of GDP is necessarily an expense, it tends to overestimate the economic weight of countries with a high public expenditure, and that are thus highly indebted. This theme is of extraordinary current relevance, not so much in its technicalities (it is not simple, and perhaps not even appropriate, to remove public sector services from GDP), but more for the importance of counting public debt together with GDP for the purpose of creating indicators that are capable of giving a more precise idea of a country's wealth.

From a historical point of view we should note that GDP as we know it today is a relatively recent concept, since it is linked to the development of national accounting dating from the 1930s (the work of Simon Kuznets was important in this regard). What is rarely discussed however is that its real founding fathers (or grand-fathers) were the so-called *économistes*, that is, the Physiocrats, who were French scholars of various disciplinary origins active in the middle of the eighteenth century. Their intellectual leader was the court physician François Quesnay (1694–1774), who proposed the well-known *Tableau économique* model. They argued that the economic power of a country is not measured by the value of its goods stocks, but by its economic flows, by *revenue* (this was different from the mercantilist school, which measured the wealth of a nation primarily on the basis of the gold it held). That is, it is not the measure of wealth in terms of lands, raw materials, labour, capital and stocks of all sorts that makes a people "rich", but the capacity of that people to make those various forms of capital circulate so as to generate revenue. Indeed, we know today that if a people is not capable of putting those funds, lands and capital to use to generate revenue, it is not wealthy but indigent, even if they are sitting on gold mines (as the past and recent history of humanity tells us).

From the Physiocrats onward, the annual flow of wealth – which they called *produit net* (net product) and which we today call "national revenue" (measured by various techniques) – tells us the wealth of a nation. Adam Smith also noted this in the opening lines of *The Wealth of Nations*:

The annual labour of every nation is the fund which originally supplies it with all the necessaries and convenien-
cies of life which it annually consumes, and which consist
always either in the immediate produce of that labour, or
in what is purchased with that produce from other nations.
(Smith [1776] 1981: 10)

In this text the key word is "annual", not "fund" (which was the legacy of the mercantilist culture), just as it is crucial that the source of that value is human labour.

Actually, the most serious current criticism of GDP is not its (overemphasized) inadequacy to measure human well-being, much less happiness (no serious economist ever thought that), but its *obsolescence*. Technical aspects on how public expenditure is calculated, how the "basket of goods" is formed, price indexes and so forth would now require rapidly updating, with significant modifications.

In this regard Fuà's words from his *Crescita economica* are relevant today: "I am convinced that the experts who founded political economy as an autonomous discipline did well in choosing the quantity of goods produced as a central theme of the new discipline" (Fuà 1993: 106). However, in much of the world today that flow of goods (GDP) is no longer adequate to express economic well-being, since "to achieve this task in wealthy countries we must stop privileging the traditional theme of the quantity of goods produced and give greater attention to other themes that can no longer be considered secondary from the point of view of economic well-being" (*ibid*.: 107). For Fuà one of these themes was worker satisfaction. For us today a crucial theme is relationships, relational goods and social capital. On the occasion of being awarded an honorary degree by the University of Urbino in 2004, the Italian economist Giacomo Becattini stated:

Well, I dream of an annual report on the state of the country ... in which – in addition to GDP, which allows comparisons in time and space, although more in appearance than in reality – we are provided with a whole battery of indicators that give us an idea how people are living in various places, as well as the morale of the various peoples, and in which the structure of the productive process of well-being is minutely described, and perhaps modelled, for every place in the country.

Beyond GDP: but how and to where?

There is an even more radical criticism of GDP, rarely emphasized by its critics, that takes us back to its eighteenth-century origins. The idea that the measures of real wealth are not based on capital stocks, but on flows or revenue, may mislead us today. Although we want to continue giving value to an indicator for economic flows – such as an updated and renewed GDP – in the era of common goods (the commons) that we have dramatically entered in this third millennium, capital stocks once again occupy the centre of the economic, social and political stage. Why? The environment, relationships, social themes such as migration, inclusivity and terrorism, as well as those themes that have become central in this era of common goods, are matters of stocks and forms of capital, not flows. Rather, revenue flows, including the large financial flows that to a large extent dominate the real flows of goods and services, are producing serious effects on our planet's stocks. We urgently need new indicators of ancient and new forms of capital.[2]

2. Or, instead of "capital", perhaps new indicators of "heritages", an evocative and less ideologically loaded term symbolically understood as the *patres-munus* – the gift of our fathers – we have received from past generations that we must safeguard and develop.

We must learn to adequately measure our environmental, relational, human (understood in a meta-economic sense), cultural and spiritual heritage, which today are forms of capital that, along with non-renewable energy sources, are subjected to deep changes (frequently, although not always, negative) precisely due to the large scale intrusion of revenue flows, as measured by GDP.

What then should we do? We will limit ourselves to pointing out five directions for action. We should:

- Bring the techniques for measuring GDP up to date, which are no longer adequate to account for wealth that is increasingly immaterial and tied less to goods;
- Strengthen the current attempts being made to define quantitative summary indicators complementary to GDP (if we want to leave GDP as an improved indicator of economic well-being) that focus on other dimensions, primarily environmental and relational, of well-being. This proposal requires focusing on capital stocks, with techniques closer to those used for taking a census than those used today for GDP;
- Do this in such a way that these new indicators measure not only or predominately flows, but stocks, capital and heritages, turning to appropriate measuring techniques – which cannot be those used for GDP – based on questionnaires or focus groups, something analogous to what is happening today with international metrics of subjective happiness;
- Work along the methodological direction indicated by Becattini and his invitation to "return to the local territory". In contrast with GDP, which is based on individuals, these civil heritages should be based on *places*, because the basic unit adequate for studying relationships can be neither the individual nor companies, but the "concerted productivity" of territories. Indeed, value is not the result of either companies or individuals

in and of themselves, but rather of the "concert" of places where there are many performers and protagonists.

- Finally, there is a more general question of a cultural and political nature. Even if new indicators complementary to GDP are created, which is appropriate, there would need to be a cultural change such that they could be recognized and taken seriously. This must begin with companies and the business community. As long as the sole indicators of a company's success (in particular, large companies) are profits earned, and as long as the "social balances" are contained in glossy brochures given to stakeholders during corporate gatherings, without these balances having any relevance for the important questions such as the appointment of new managers and board members, it will be impossible for our culture to come to appreciate and value indicators other than GDP. It is a question of culture, for which the only solution is to start with daily routines, which is always the basis for epochal changes. Therefore, a serious polity that wants to go beyond GDP towards "public happiness" must be accompanied by a culture and practice that, for example, changed the nature and scope of social balances.

Gross, as in dirty?

GDP does not measure much, and many of the things it does measure it measures badly; we have already said that. But, we have never considered eliminating GDP to replace it with other indicators of well-being because, although democracy has a growing need for more socio-economic indicators, it is still important to have an indicator of a country's production of goods and services. GDP is full of data that tells us little about our well-being, or that tells us more about the opposite (for example, games of chance and many other things, as we have seen). Until now, all this ethically discordant quantity of data referenced (or we hoped it referenced) legitimate economic activity within the law. However, the Eurostat has recently decided (and as silent citizens we are therefore complicit) that GDP should include estimates of criminal activity, such as drug trafficking and the exploitation of human trafficking in prostitution. With this civilly atrocious change, GDP has lost all contact with civilization and the common good. GDP was already in trouble, considering the number of moral and civil "bads" that were included in it, but now the divorce between GDP and civility is practically complete. And we are all the poorer for it, because someone (who?) maladroitly thought to broaden the techniques for calculating GDP, which have been silently accommodated.

Today we no longer draw anything substantial from the variations in that indicator, and it has become a useless exercise to celebrate its positive growth rate. This is why we economists should be the first to be saddened by this historic turn; instead we, as a profession that is all too often glaringly cynical, dismiss these objections as arguments by nostalgic moralists who are naive and not very bright, rather than protest that GDP as we are making it is losing all contact with the grand tradition of economic science. This is true not only of Antonio Genovesi's civil economy, obviously, but also with that of Adam Smith, which has always been a tradition that considered the production of goods and services on the whole as ethically good. Today those who do not firmly protest this uncivil innovation are in fact ratifying and approving of the economy's exit from the good things of our common life. With this shift it is very worrying to see just how low the civil and economic culture of our technical experts and high bureaucrats has fallen.

Statistics, a noble art of social well-being, has always had a very rich humanistic tradition in Italy. The Milanese economist Melchiorre Gioia, one of the founders of modern statistics, and another civil economist who continued Dragonetti's tradition of virtues and rewards, considered it an integrating part of the civilizing process. Statistics is a mirror of a country's culture because with it we measure something we want to *see*, on the basis of a civilization and an idea of the common good. Whoever introduced this modification in GDP is making no distinction in nature between an entrepreneur who produces and pays taxes and a Mafia entrepreneur who doesn't, between those who hire and those who make people work in the black market, between those who respect the law and those who reject it. This innovation renounces centuries of tradition and humanist statistics; it offends those who work and live legally. But our technical experts lack the culture and history to be able to recognize this; the spectacle of the destruction of our European civilization continues in the silence typical of epochal devastation. We continue to humiliate honesty and virtue and serve vices and the dishonest, and in so doing actually give them scientific dignity.

We are certain that something will change in the near future. The statement made by William Dudley, president of the Federal Reserve Bank of New York, is encouraging:

In recent years, there have been ongoing occurrences of serious professional misbehaviour, ethical lapses and compliance failures at financial institutions. ... The pattern of bad behaviour did not end with the financial crisis, but continued despite the considerable public sector intervention that was necessary to stabilize the financial system. ... Ethical problems in organizations originate not with 'a few bad apples' but with the 'barrel makers'. That is, the problems originate from the culture of the firms, and this culture is largely shaped by the firms' leadership. This means that the solution needs to originate from within the firms, from their leaders. What do

I mean by the culture within a firm? Culture relates to the implicit norms that guide behavior in the absence of regulations or compliance rules – and sometimes despite those explicit restraints.

(Dudley 2014)

We should never take for granted that such a high level banker can talk about the "cultural bankruptcy of Wall Street"!

What Dudley and other influential bankers, such as Mark Carney, the governor of the Bank of England, are saying is that the economy does not gain prestige due to its therapeutic efficiency (as is the case in medicine), but from the idea that the economy itself establishes the reality that politicians and citizens must measure up to. And the place in which values – what is good, true and right – are defined is the financial market. It does not take much effort to understand that this is bad epistemology, because, contrary to what the mainstream preaches, there are not just facts, but interpretations as well. A reasonable hermeneutic is therefore urgent, because the rationality of mathematical and econometric modelling is not enough.

There are many signs that the notion of social well-being, riding the wave of many different events, is today having a sort of reawakening with renewed interest in it, and this gives a reason for hope. We need not be surprised: once we acknowledge the looming crisis of civilization, we are almost propelled to abandon all dystopian attitudes, daring to try new ways of thought and action.

7

Common goods

Of plenty there is enough; what is lacking is the little.

– Epicurus

The question of common goods, or the commons, is one against which to test the robustness of the conceptual framework of the civil economy. Interest in this question has grown dramatically over the last few decades, even though the first systematic reflection in economics goes back to 1911, when Katherine Coman published "Some Unsettled Problems of Irrigation" in the *American Economic Review*. However, in discussing alternate forms of property in the *Politics* Aristotle had already made specific reference to common goods: "It is clearly better that property should be private, but the use of it common; and the special business of the legislator is to create in men this benevolent disposition" (II.5.37).

Goods such as air, water, climate, soil fertility, biodiversity, seeds and knowledge are posing hitherto unforeseen challenges for the future of humanity, in that they are essential goods for which it is practically impossible to find substitutes. Common goods have always existed, but only in recent times has it been acknowledged that there is a problem of determining the limit beyond which we begin consuming "tragedy". The term is taken from Garrett Hardin, an American biologist, who in 1968 published "The Tragedy of the Commons", an article that made him famous. Clearly, Hardin could not have imagined the heated debates that his essay unleashed. First, because not all types of common goods lead to the tragedy of depletion. That happens when one considers – as did Hardin – only rivalry in consumption and non-excludability of use as characteristic aspects of the common good. For example, in his 2012 book *Infrastructure*, Brett M. Frischmann talks about the *comedy* of commons to emphasize that *open access* generates positive externalities that are never counted in economic calculations.

Second, because the word "tragedy" creates misconceptions. In common use it indicates "ruin", or "inauspicious outcome", while Hardin used the term to denote a situation similar to the prisoner's dilemma, in which the optimal solution cannot obtain as long as the agents act according to the standard of *homo economicus*. A social dilemma describes a state of affairs in which there is a radical conflict between individual interest and collective interest, as Hardin's example of grazing land makes very clear. In such situations it is vain for mainstream economics to look for a solution, as it tries so hard to do, within the limits of its technical toolkit. That is not difficult to grasp.

A society in which each person pursues her own self-interest normally works well because citizens caring for their own interests is an expression of civil virtue. As we have already noted, this idea underlies the most famous metaphor of economic science, the Smithian "invisible hand": each person pursues his private interests while respecting the rules of the competitive game, and society providentially finds itself with the common good as well. However, there is a serious problem: the ethical legitimization of exchange and this virtuous vision of self-interest (understood as prudence) function only in societies that are so simple that the good of the individual is directly the good of all. This happens where goods are predominately private, such as food, housing, cars, and so forth. Where common goods are present (which become more numerous and important as a society slowly evolves) prudence is no longer automatically a market virtue since it is no longer true that private interest also produces the common good; rather, individual good produces the common bad.

One of the most notable changes in a globalized, postmodern society therefore concerns common goods, which are now the rule and no longer the exception. Indeed, today the quality and sustainability of the development process of various emerging countries certainly depends on the classic private and public goods, but much more on the common goods or bads. One need only consider the environment or nature reserves to find confirmation of that.

The nature of the commons

What does it mean to adopt the civil economy point of view regarding the commons? It means understanding that the nature of a common good is such that the advantage or benefit that each person draws from its use cannot be separated from the advantage that others also draw from it. That is to say that the benefit that the individual receives from the good in question is enjoyed *together* with that of others, and neither *against* them – as happens with private goods – nor *excluding* them – as happens with public goods.

What is the practical implication of this? One can solve the problem of private goods by recourse to the principle of exchange between peers; and the problem of public goods can be solved by recourse to the principle of redistribution, entrusting the task of determining their quantity and use to the public authority. In the case of common goods, the only principle in which to take recourse is *reciprocity*. And herein lies the crux of the problem. Contemporary economic culture has so forgotten the category of reciprocity that there is not even the slightest hint that common goods can ever be appropriately managed by private or public means, but only by communal means (though not communitarian).

Only by taking a step back from libertarian individualism – although without rejecting its important achievements – can an economy be open to a relational dimension, and thus capable of suggesting interventions and specific actions adequate to resolve the "tragedy" of the commons. Hannah Arendt (1906–75) understood this point better than others. In her 1958 work *The Human Condition* she wrote that what is public, or common, is what is in the light, or that which can be seen and discussed: "Everything that appears in public can be seen and heard by everybody" (Arendt [1958] 1998: 50). What is private, to the contrary, is what is removed from sight: "the term 'public' signifies the world itself, in so far as it is common to all of us and distinguished from our privately owned place in it" (*ibid.*: 52).

Ultimately, what is at the heart of the tragedy of the commons is that individuals follow their own short-sighted and self-interested pursuits, which leads them – although without intention – to cut off the branch they are sitting on. Hardin's example of the common grazing land where each farmer leads her own animals to graze illustrates the idea well: rational choice, which leads one to maximize one's individual interest, suggests that each farmer increase her herd by one animal, because by so doing she gains, say, x, while the availability of grass decreases by only a fraction of x, since the consequent damage is divided among the other $n - 1$ farmers.

It is as if those using the pasture, at the moment of acting, were not taking into account the reduction in the common good (the pasture grass) entailed by their choice. This happens because each person sees only his individual interest; that is, each one sees only himself, and is thus, literally, an *idiótes*.[1] With agents who are *idiótai*, it is not difficult to understand why sooner or later the threshold will be crossed beyond which they will consume tragedy. When that happens people hasten to hoard or exploit the resource even more, precisely because it becomes more scarce.

What then are the possible solutions to the problem of the commons? The two classic solutions are the social contract *à la* Hobbes (creating an artificial pact, a Leviathan) and individual ethics. The Hobbesian solution entrusts the state with the task of creating a system of rules and sanctions for those who break the rules. Then rational, self-interested agents understand that if they themselves do not limit their own freedom, they cannot avoid tragedy and the negative consequences that follow from it. Apart from the high price of the loss of individual liberty imposed by signing a social contract, the chief limitation to such a solution today is that with global commons, which are increasingly relevant, there is (fortunately!) no possibility of giving life to a Leviathan on the same scale. Who could ever create an enforcement system for the agreements the great world powers would eventually stipulate? The failures of the accords on CO_2 emissions, exploiting the ocean floors and climate change eloquently confirm this.

The other solution, which can also be a reaction of distrust to top-down solutions, depends instead on individual ethics of a Kantian or Humean sort. Agents would internalize ethical norms – say, do not pollute the environment – and follow them because

---

1. In classical Greek the word has the sense of a private or a political citizen as opposed to the state or a government official (see "ιδηωτ-εια" and its "-ησ" subentry in Liddell & Scott 1968). In his well-known work *The Peloponnesian Wars* the Greek historian Thucydides referenced the speech by the Athenian statesman Pericles in the fifth century BCE, in which he stated that a democracy can never work for long if the majority of citizens act like *idiótai*. And indeed, democracy is a common good.

they would know that in so doing they would make things easier, in the sense that they would be better able to achieve their life goals. Technically, it would be as if individuals modified their preference systems to the point of including the commons in their own objective functions. By so doing the common good also becomes a private good, thanks to internal sanctions and rewards. Appearances notwithstanding, this solution in and of itself is complementary, rather than an alternative, to the Hobbesian solution; neither is its complementarity automatic, due to the frequent phenomena of crowding out: the external motivators of sanctions levied by the Leviathan would crowd out the internal motivations of individual ethics.

Individual ethics is certainly important and co-essential, but they are not sufficient, particularly during our current historical period. The reason is that it is centred around the individual, just as Hobbes's solution was centred around the state. What is missing in both is civil society, which is neither state nor capitalist market, nor is it an integral summation of individual and private affairs. What we gain from the perspective of the civil economy is the understanding that "culture" does not mean merely changing individuals' values, but moving to a different perception of the problem, to a "common" vision that focuses on "we". A typical reasoning process of someone who looks on the world from the perspective of "we" is "better me than no one". Even knowing the risk of being taken advantage of by free riding, that is, by others' opportunism, I decide to contribute to the common good because I know that my actions have some chance of stimulating others' reciprocity (we must never forget that reciprocity is innate in the human person, even though with lack of practice it can atrophy).

How many "we-actors" must there be to bring about the desired outcome? Findings from current experimental economics and research in the neurosciences indicate that if two key conditions are satisfied, even a small percentage of "we-actors" is capable of infectiously influencing a large population. First, the "prophetic minority", as it is called in the literature, do not become discouraged after their first actions, that is, that they know how to persist, and second, that the "we-actors" have a degree of sophistication in being able to explain to free riders the unreasonableness of their individualistic behaviour, not with sermons or appeal to their moral senses, but by factually demonstrating the incremental gains that the "we-rationality" strategy can guarantee. Is it not perhaps true that the great epochal changes in history are nearly always the result of the actions of a prophetic minority?

To avoid any misunderstanding, we want to point out that this does not mean that government leaders (or their electorate, who too often are not very far-sighted) should do all they can to arrive at global agreements with sanctions; as previously noted, this is not a navigable course. Rather, we hold that it is urgently necessary to put the civil society to work, organized to achieve a global social compact among free and equal citizens who adopt a "we" culture. This would be a *compact*, in contrast to a Hobbesian *contract*, which tends to be illiberal, or a contract signed by "chiefs", whether of a government, family or clan. This must be a compact of fraternity, following equality and liberty. The latter two are the triumph of modernity; they have created a new democracy and established rights, but they are showing themselves incapable of managing common goods. *Liberté* and *égalité* speak of the individual; *fraternité* is the principle of modernity that speaks to *bonds* between persons. Without bonds, and without recognizing ourselves to be bound to one another, because we have need of the same common resources, we will never be able to escape the tragedy of the commons.

Managing common goods

Now we can understand why neither private nor public management of common goods are able to produce the desired effects. Let us first consider the private solution. As has been noted, it avails itself of market mechanisms to suggest how to best manage the good under consideration. But that mechanism presupposes that there is freedom of choice on both the supply and demand sides. In the case of essential goods – water, air, seeds, and so forth – while there is freedom to sell them, there is no analogous freedom to acquire them, for the obvious reason that the goods that are essential for life have no substitutes. It follows that artificially making common goods private thoroughly undermines the operation of the market. Note the analogy with what happens when a monopoly disrupts a market because it impedes exercising the freedom to sell (see Zamagni 2015).

Indeed, we should not forget that one of the fundamental characteristics of capitalist markets is that they do not satisfy needs, but preferences that can be paid. I may be thirsty to the point of death, but if I have no means of paying, my need certainly cannot be satisfied. Not only that, but the market is an institution that, in and of itself, is incapable of distinguishing between ethically-grounded preferences and mere desires. Precisely because this institution is not capable of discerning between legitimate and illegitimate motives, it cannot fulfil the role of a court to which we can entrust the defence of values such as positive liberty. The existence of this radial asymmetry between the supply and demand of an essential good is what makes a private solution problematic. This sort of asymmetry reduces the capabilities – in Amartya Sen's sense – of economically-marginalized agents. Keep in mind that a person who does not have access to certain basic goods cannot avail himself of a value such as liberty.

In short, the transformation of commons into commodities (which tends to follow with privatization) in no way resolves the problem, because the tragedy of the commons is not due to a problem of property rights allocation, as many continue to erroneously believe. It is rather a problem of governance, that is, a problem that regards the allocation of control rights. The possible presence of regulatory public authorities does not change this judgement. This is true even in light of the fact that the "private property, private management" model for common goods – the so-called "cap and trade" model – is subject to well-known phenomena of regulator capture[2] by those who are bound to respect the laws.

What should we say of the opposite solution of making common goods public? Despite appearances, we must recognize that this is not a navigable course, because transforming a common good into a public good would distort its very nature. Indeed, goods that a long historical tradition had exempted from private appropriation and utilization were later drawn into the system of landlord ("*dominicale*") rights as a sort of public property; among these, in Italy, were participatory agriculture ("*partecipanze agrarie*") in Emilia, alpine associations ("*comunanze alpine*"), and the *Regole di Cortina* (a system of shared commons management) that hearken back to 1241. There are specific reasons to reinforce this judgement. The first regards the problem of finance. For example, consider the case of the water system in Italy; it is a real "sieve", in the succinct definition of the Centro Studi Investimenti Sociali (Centre for the Study of Social Investments, www.censis.it), that loses around 47 per cent of its water – water that is wasted due to the lack of necessary investment to maintain water plants and pipelines. The result is that the cost of using such an essential good is among the highest

---

2. Regulator capture is a form of corruption that occurs when a regulatory agency, created to act in the public interest, identifies with the interest of the industry they are supposed to regulate.

in Europe (the average European loss is around 13 per cent), despite the fact that according to Eurostat data Italy has around 300 billion cubic meters of rainfall; water is not a scarce good in Italy. The fact is that the financial resources necessary to construct a water system able to conserve water and to maintain its distribution system are beyond the public budget.

There is a second reason for the unsustainability of the public solution. The literature, which is by now significant, on government failures has shown that the actions of the public system, whether central or local, are affected by two specific afflictions: bureaucracy and rent-seeking. These characteristics make nationalization inefficient and ultimately unsustainable, even setting aside the financing difficulties just discussed and the cancer of corruption.

This is why the communal solution offers the best chances for exiting the tragedy of the commons. What in fact is missing from the private and public solutions is the idea of community. If those who use a common good do not recognize (and accept) that a bond of reciprocity exists between them, neither the Hobbesian social contract, which entrusts the task of averting the risk of exclusion to the Leviathan, nor liberal individualism, which entrusts the task of self-limitation to individual consciences, can ever constitute satisfying solutions for the problem of common goods. These goods have widespread ownership in the exact sense that everyone must be able to access them. It follows that access and property are clearly distinct categories, and sometimes in conflict; this is true even setting aside whether property is public or private. The basic idea, which was first rigorously explored by Elinor Ostrom in her work *Governing the Commons* (1990), is to put the creativity of civil society to work to invent original forms of communal management, because the management model must be consistent with the very nature of the good under discussion: if it is common, then its management must also be common.

In current historical conditions the type of commons management that is showing itself to be the most practical is cooperation. However, this is not the mono-stakeholder type of cooperative, which would not give adequate assurances in this regard. We must instead think of the multi-stakeholder model of cooperative if we want to create an optimal supply-side organization for the common good. This model is not yet widespread, even though the experiences of the social cooperatives that emerged in the early 1970s, and the recent emergence of community cooperatives, are significant precedents for attaining an institutional model suitable for overcoming the tragedy of the commons. The cooperative solution allows us to give the necessary attention to the demand side of common goods, which until now has been systematically overlooked. Official economic theory has always privileged the supply-side approach to the problems of the commons; that effectively says we are always concerned with ways to recover costs and preserve the incentives that guarantee adequate supply levels. A demand theory of common goods has been developed, however: the consumer of common goods is a passive subject that "should" consume what the supply side decides to offer. This is a lapse in official theory of no small account; while an articulated demand theory of private and public goods has been developed, this is not the case for common goods. And yet, the demand for common goods is continually growing in our societies.

We are persuaded that a credible and shared solution to the problem under discussion will not be found until we give a central place to the "excluded middle", that is, the civil society and its economic expressions. After all, why should we not consider solutions for the management of common goods – primarily water – similar to those historically employed for medical care, poverty and aid? A few decades ago these spheres, which are other forms of common goods, were totally in the hands of the state and/or families. Today, in large measure these social services are in the hands of thousands of cooperatives and social enterprises. Civil society has always had civil entrepreneurs who, without expecting large returns on their investments, have wanted, and know how to, use their talents to manage common goods. We need civil entrepreneurs, not bureaucrats, to face up to the challenges of the commons.

There have been moments in our history when communities, societies and peoples have been at the crossroads that divides fraternity from fratricide, two roads that have always been intertwined since the time of Cain and then Romulus. At times fraternity has been the chosen direction; more frequently, the choice has been towards fratricide. Today we are at this crossroads. The very future of our species is at stake, but we still have time to take the right path, provided that we recognize that true reciprocity emerges only by admitting our mutual vulnerability. We must recognize that we can exit the tragedy of the commons only by accepting and suffering the small, daily instances of betrayed reciprocity and lack of response by others; these are the "good pains" the American philosopher Martha Nussbaum discussed in her work *The Fragility of Goodness* (1986), on which a flourishing life ultimately depends.

8

Towards civil welfare

Roses have thorns, and silver fountains mud.
                              – Shakespeare, Sonnet 35

In 1919 several great industrialists in the United States, among them David Rockefeller, Henry Ford and Andrew Carnegie, signed an agreement that launched an initiative that shortly afterward would be called *welfare capitalism*. On the strength of the restitution principle, the basic assumption of this agreement envisaged that companies should take responsibility for the well-being of their dependents and their families. In this way the company gives back a part of the profits that resulted from those who competed to create them. This is a typical principle of American cultural origin: to give back *post factum* (after the fact) a part of what was obtained thanks to the contribution of the community that contributed to the successful implementation of a productive activity. Welfare capitalism immediately had some success in the United States, but it did not take long for its Achilles heel to become evident: it did not satisfy the requirement of universalism. The compact did not have value *erga omnes* (for everyone), since it was a private action on a voluntary basis.[1] This is why, exactly twenty years later in Britain, the liberal John Maynard Keynes wrote that if welfare is desired as the model of social order, it can only be universal (Keynes 1939). Indeed, a particularistic welfare would not guarantee social peace, neither would it serve to reduce inequality. Thanks to this insight, Lord Beveridge, a member of the British Parliament, succeeded in having the famous "Beveridge Report" approved during wartime in 1942. From this were launched the National Health Service, free assistance to the handicapped and elderly who were not self-sufficient, and free education for all until a certain age. This was the beginning in Britain of the famous model of the *welfare state*: the state, not the company, must take care of the well-being of its citizens by putting the principle of redistribution into practice.[2] Beveridge's phrase has become famous: the state must take responsibility for citizens "from cradle to grave". This model represented an authentic triumph of civilization, which then spread from Britain to the rest of Europe, in different versions and with different outcomes. This did not happen in the United States, where the welfare state never took root. There, welfare capitalism became more robust over the years with the growth of non-profit organizations, which maintained a special relationship with the for-profit world (one need only consider that nearly all American philanthropic foundations bear the names of their founders). Americans would give up this model only with great difficulty.

Nonetheless, over the course of the last quarter century the welfare state model has begun to show serious stress points,

---

1. A recent example of such a model is the "Giving Pledge" project promoted in the United States by Bill Gates and Warren Buffett; at this point about fifty billionaires have pledged to give up to 50 per cent of their wealth to socially relevant causes.

2. A few singular institutions, such as obligatory insurance, had already been introduced since the end of the nineteenth century in countries such as Germany, Sweden and even Italy.

revealing a double weakness. The first is financial sustainability. If welfare services are to retain their quality they must keep pace with scientific and technological progress; costs grow over time, and the primary means the state has at its disposal to cover those costs is general taxation. Keeping the tax level high enough to cover the entire expense would require unsustainably high levels of fiscal pressure. It is evident that if the resources to finance the welfare state had to come exclusively from general taxation – and potentially from sales or excise taxes – the mounting fiscal pressure would end up putting the country's democratic system itself at risk. Note that the growing divergence between the curve that represents welfare costs over time, due primarily to healthcare and assistance, and the curve that represents tax revenue over time would exist even if, by some fortuitous chance, tax evasion, waste and corruption could be eliminated. The divergence would be smaller, but the problem of bloat in the public budget would remain unchanged.

The second main weakness in the welfare state is the bureaucratization of the system. We use the word "bureaucratization" in a technical sense to mean standardizing the ways of meeting needs. The problem is that people's needs cannot be standardized. There is by now a vast array of examples that explain the asymmetry between the diversity of human needs and having them met by the public authority, which requires uniformity. That is why social services are surrounded by an aura of discontent. The low view of public services by citizens is, in Italy for example, tightly linked to the lack of tacit quality, although the codified quality is adequate. As the philosopher Michael Polanyi (1891–1976) made clear, "codified" quality can be controlled and guaranteed by a third party with respect to the service supplier and the person in need; an example might be a government inspector. "Tacit" quality is instead the quality that can be ascertained only by the one receiving the service, who alone can judge whether the service was provided in a relational manner or not.

One question naturally arises: why are welfare state services provided impersonally? The reason is contractualism, specifically its social contract form, which is the theoretical base that upheld and legitimized the welfare state from its very beginning in advanced Western countries. Just as the private contract is the nexus of market transactions between economic agents, in the same way the social contract gives a foundation to the "well-ordered society" that John Rawls discussed in his 1971 work *A Theory of Justice*. What do we find underlying the idea of a contract, whether private or social? The notion of "negotiability": to pursue their own ends in the best possible way, rational self-interested subjects find it convenient to subscribe to a contract that fixes obligations and advantages for each of the parties in question. The conception in which personal interest underlies the social contract entails that the rights invoked by the contracting parties derive from the ability of all to pursue their own interest. That effectively says that a person acquires, say, the right to property if he has the capacity or faculty to have property. At the same time, a right cannot be adequately exercised if the person in question does not have the ability to contract – a principle that John Locke had already foreseen at the end of the seventeenth century.

But what about those who, being neither independent nor self-sufficient, for example, those who are disabled, are not able to negotiate and thus are not able to subscribe to the social contract? That is, what about the outliers who cannot participate in the negotiation process because they have nothing to offer in exchange? As the Canadian–American philosopher David Gauthier, a Rawlsian contractualist, admitted with admirable intellectual honesty:

> The primary problem is care for the handicapped. Speaking euphemistically of enabling them to live productive lives, when the services required exceed any possible product,

conceals an issue which, understandably, no one wants to face. ... Such persons are not party to the moral relationships grounded by a contractarian theory.

(Gauthier 1986: 18, and n. 30)

In other words, since for contractualism all rights originate in the social contract, if a person cannot take part because she lacks the ability to contract, and no one agrees to represent her, she will not enjoy the services guaranteed to those who participated in the contractual process. In short, political theories based on the social contract, inasmuch as they deny reference to something that lies outside the contract, are able to explain communal life, but they cannot explain why it is *good* that people exist and why it is *good* that they continue to exist.

Recognizing ourselves as mutually vulnerable

When we reach this stage of awareness, we understand why it is necessary to find a new ethical basis for welfare. A "decent" society (which in Avishai Margalit's sense is a society that does not humiliate its members by making them feel irrelevant or redundant) cannot consent that the excluded should be offered either state paternalism or anyone's pity. We need a more original and robust principle than that of negotiability if we want to overcome contractualism's aporias. What might it be? The civil economy's response offers the principle of vulnerability in the sense given by Martha Nussbaum. Accepting reciprocal dependence, and thus the "symmetry of needs", follows from recognizing vulnerability as a signature aspect of the human condition. Taking care of the other thus becomes an expression of the need to offer care, that is, the need to reciprocate the gesture or help one has received. It is clear that the social bond that originates from accepting the principle of vulnerability is far more robust than one originating from a contract.

Accepting this principle entails surpassing the concept of fragility. The welfare state is centred around fragility, but that is not enough. In a technical sense someone is "vulnerable" who has a high probability of falling into a situation of fragility in a relatively short span of time – say, one year. I may not be fragile today, but if by a series of circumstances I have a high probability of becoming fragile over a certain arc of time, I must be considered vulnerable. The shift from a fragility welfare to a vulnerability welfare is a welfare that stays a step ahead of the game, which in the end saves resources. It is a little like what can happen with one's health: if I do not have check-ups with a certain regularity, and I am then diagnosed with a serious disease, I end up costing the public health system much more.

But there is more. Thinking about welfare in terms of mutual vulnerability allows us to understand that the real limit of the welfare state is the practical impossibility of delivering what it promises. We know that the welfare state was immediately met with great favour because, as Aristotle had anticipated, democracy presupposes a certain degree of equality between citizens in order to work. So, we can choose one or the other: either reduce inequality or reduce the space of democratic practice. US President James Madison, writing in the *Federalist Papers* (1788), preferred the latter; however, continuing along that line in the twentieth century would have been too dangerous for public order, and with good reason. The ultimate sense of the welfare state was that of having made the capitalist market economy socially and politically acceptable. Reduction in inequality and recognition of the rights of citizenship are needed to guarantee growth without excessive social tensions. To the invisible hand of the market the visible (and heavy) hand of the state is added.

However, the advent of globalization at the end of the 1970s radically changed the picture.[3] Inequality in income distribution and total assets increased disproportionately with respect to the increase in income at the trans-national and intra-national levels, as is evident from the work of Branko Milanovic and Thomas Piketty. That all happened without diminishing social public spending. Quite the contrary. Consider that in Italy, even today over 50 per cent of GDP is generated from the public sector, and social public spending has continued to increase in the last few decades, except during the recent crisis years. This means that the welfare state is not protecting the most vulnerable, nor is it facilitating the mobility of those on the lowest rungs of the social ladder. Inequality, therefore, is not so much the result of penury as it is of the presence of economic institutions that absorb the excess produced in the economy and turn it into rents, which are always parasitic. This is why growth in and of itself is no longer a guarantee of reduced inequality.

So what is at the root of the "failure" of the welfare state? It is that the model is built on the fallacious presupposition that first one needs to make the "pie" bigger, before (re)allocating it justly. This is the source of the well-known division of roles: the capitalist market is asked to produce the most wealth possible, within the limits of resources and technology, without worrying much about how it is obtained (because "business is business" and "competition is competition", as if to say that the ethical dimension has nothing to do with the time when wealth is produced). The state then has the task of seeing to the redistribution of produced wealth according to some criterion of fairness. The great French economist Léon Walras (1834–1910) had already sought to criticize this view at the end of the nineteenth century: "When you set yourselves to redistribute

---

3. The process of globalization "officially" began at the first Group of Six (G6) summit at Rambouillet, Paris, in November 1975.

the pie you will not be able redistribute the injustices committed to make it larger."

We are now able to grasp the real limit of the welfare state, which is that it implicitly accepts that the capitalist market should fully follow its own logic, except that the state then enters after the fact with ad hoc interventions to mitigate its harmful effects – without touching the system, however. Note that this is the heart of the reformist strategy: undesired effects are corrected, but without interfering, except marginally, in the processes that cause them. This way of visualizing the problem has produced negative consequences at the cultural level as well, by making scholars and policy-makers accept that ethics, while having something to say about the *distribution* of income and wealth, should have nothing to do with the *production* process because it is governed by the Millian iron laws of the market. Having legitimized the separation (which is very different from the distinction) between the economic and social spheres – assigning the first the task of producing as much wealth as possible, and then assigning the second the task of redistributing it – has been the chief limit of the welfare state. This has brought about the belief that a democratic society can progress by keeping separate the rules of efficiency and solidarity, regulating relationships in the former only within the sphere of the market, and applying the latter exclusively in the social sphere. Hence the source of the paradox that afflicts our societies: on the one hand people increasingly take positions in favour of the disabled, the unemployed, and those who are left behind in market competition; on the other, the entire system of values (the criteria for evaluating individual actions and lifestyles) is centred around the principle of efficiency, which has become the real principle of reality. This is the source of the contrast between the respect due to individuals as persons, thus essentially different, and the respect due them as human beings, and thus essentially equal.

Should we be surprised if today the indicators of public happiness constantly decline while various types of inequality continually rise? Should we be surprised if the principle of meritoriousness is (clumsily) confused with meritocracy, as if they were synonyms? (And to think that Aristotle was the first to write that a meritocracy is dangerous for democracy.) What's more, should we be surprised if the endemic increase in inequality elicits rebuffs from citizens in the face of such a troubling phenomenon? To the contrary, the by now accepted belief that elitism should be encouraged so that the well-being of the many could grow by supporting the abilities of the few, through various incentives and resources, is taken as incontrovertible truth. The result is that excluding the less gifted and thus less productive from the production process becomes not just normal, but necessary, if we want society to progress. The trickle-down effect will ensure that a few drops of well-being reach the excluded, since "a rising tide lifts all boats"! No more misleading, to say nothing of erroneous, aphorism could be coined.

Civil welfare and circular subsidiarity

The systemic – not merely situational – crisis in the welfare state has brought about a growing interest in the civil welfare model. In the civil welfare model, the entire society, and not just the state, must take responsibility for those that live in it. In parallel to this idea, the principle of *circular subsidiarity* has emerged. If society as a whole should take care of all those who live in it, without exclusions of any kind, it is clear that it is necessary to bring together the three spheres that make up the whole of society: the sphere of public authorities (the state, regions, communities, and various para-state entities), the corporate sphere (the business community), and the sphere of organized civil society (various associations, social cooperatives, NGOs, social enterprises and foundations). The idea of circular subsidiarity is this: the three spheres must find ways to systematically (not occasionally) interact when planning and fielding interventions, as well as in managing them. A first benefit from civil welfare is overcoming the two aporias of the welfare state that we have discussed, but foremost, this model allows finding the necessary resources from the corporate world. When we say that "resources are lacking" the reference is to public resources, rather than to private resources that, on the contrary, are present and continually increasing. The point is that until now no one has thought to draw from the resources available from the corporate world in order to channel them towards supplying welfare services. On the flip side, the presence of the public authority remains fundamental in this model in order to guarantee universalism: the danger of excluding some social groups from benefiting from services must always be kept in mind. The part of civil society that continues to be called the "non-profit" or "third" sector (although it would be better to talk about civil society organizations) occupies a special place in circular subsidiarity, in that it has specific knowledge (who better than an association of volunteers to know if there are particular needs to be met in a neighbourhood?) and means of governance that are capable of raising the relational quality of services provided.

There is only one alternative to civil welfare: returning to welfare capitalism, which as we have seen is a model that entrusts meeting citizens' needs to the social sensibilities of companies in a decidedly partial manner (former British Prime Minister David Cameron's liberalization of the UK's National Health Service should be seen in this context). This is why it is urgent to enact a form of welfare in which companies, public entities and citizens' organizations concur, in proportion to their respective capabilities, in devising protocols for partnering to plan and manage interventions.

A clarification is appropriate here. We are discussing *circular* subsidiarity, not *horizontal* and/or *vertical* subsidiarity. While the latter two fit well with the welfare capitalism and welfare state models, they are not capable of supporting the civil welfare model, for reasons that are readily explained. In the two traditional forms of subsidiarity, the state *cedes* portions of its sovereignty to territorial and/or functional public entities (vertical subsidiarity) or to members of civil society as cultural actors (horizontal subsidiarity); in circular subsidiarity sovereignty is *shared*. "The state should not do what can best be done by lower level entities and members of the civil society" is the slogan of vertical and horizontal subsidiarity; "the state should work *together* with companies and non-profit actors" describes circular subsidiarity.

The reasons given so far to obstruct progress towards civil welfare are by now familiar, and we mention just a few: insufficient monetary resources; insufficient capacity in the bureaucratic and administrative systems to take on new tasks; too much diversity in the starting points among the various regions. There is certainly truth in all that, but it is not enough to explain the *fin de non-recevoir* to accepting circular subsidiarity. Rather, the real reason is the difficulty, which is basically cultural, of explaining to citizens that abandoning the neo-statist welfare model (in which the state retains a monopoly on providing services) does not mean falling into the arms of the neoliberal welfare capitalism model. Taking out the state does not necessarily imply privatization, because there is always the possibility of socialization. Put another way, "going non-public by socializing, not privatizing" is the civil welfare formula.

It is useful to recall that circular subsidiarity is an Italian idea that hearkens back to the epoch of Civic Humanism in the fifteenth century; it was successively formalized by the jurist Hugo Grotius and the philosopher Johannes Althusius. Here it is interesting to recall Althusius's definition of democracy as *consociato symbiotica* (symbiotic association). Since society is not an aggregation of separate identities, symbiosis is required between citizens and a symbiosis is needed between citizens and those who hold public office that is nourished by circular subsidiarity.

The transition from the welfare state (a redistributive welfare in which those with needs are only the objects of others' attention) to civil welfare (a generative welfare in which those with needs are active subjects) requires abandoning the binary "public–private" in favour of the trinary "public–private–civil".

We would like to close with a little-known, but highly eloquent passage by Alexis de Tocqueville in *Democracy in America*: "Despotism ... sees in the isolation of men the most certain guarantee of its own duration ... a despot easily pardons the governed for not loving him, provided they do not love each another" (Tocqueville [1835–40] 2010: 887). That is exactly right, as history teaches. The purpose of civil welfare is to avert that separation and, in so doing, oppose the emergence of new forms of despotism.

9

Socially responsible companies and consumers

For a thought to change the world, it must first change the life of the one who expresses it.

– Albert Camus, *Notebooks, 1935–59*

Opening a new factory at Pozzuoli, near Naples, on 23 April 1955, Adriano Olivetti gave a memorable speech to the workers. The following is an excerpt:

Can an industry take on *purposes*? Are these found simply in the profit index? Beyond its apparent rhythm, is there not something more fascinating, a destination, a *vocation*, even in the life of a factory? ... The Ivrea factory, although operating in an economic environment and accepting its rules, has turned its purposes and its primary preoccupations to the material, cultural and social elevation of the *place* where it was called to operate, launching that *region* towards a type of new community in which there is no substantial difference in purposes among the protagonists of its human affairs, of its history made day by day, to assure a future to the children of that land, a life more worthy of being lived.

(Olivetti [1955] 2012: 28–9; emphasis added)

At a time when it was broadly accepted that the cause–effect dynamic was sufficient to understand the world, Olivetti did not hesitate in stating that a company that wants to consider itself civilly responsible cannot avoid the question of the purpose for which something is done or considered good. It is interesting to compare Olivetti's words with those of Michael Hammer, one of the best-selling business and management authors:

> I'm saddened and offended by the idea that companies exist to enrich their owners ... That is the very least of their roles; they are far more worthy, more honourable, and more important than that. Without the vital creative force of business, our world would be impoverished beyond reckoning.
>
> (Quoted in Hevesi 2008)

If we look carefully at the debate on corporate social responsibility (CSR) today, we see a problematic framework emerging. To understand why, it is necessary to frame the new phenomenon of CSR within the ethical and civil valuation of the market economy. In fact, the theoretical and political debates around the economic–social dialectic can be subdivided into two traditional "parties": those who see the economy and markets as building up society, and those who instead consider the economy as being in endemic conflict with society. The liberal tradition of political economy is counted in the former, while the sociological tradition is in the latter. The theoreticians of liberal economics (from Adam Smith to Amartya Sen) consider the market as an expression of civil society, economic development as an indicator of social development, and economic liberty as a prerequisite for other liberties. In particular, the extension of markets and their logic becomes the *sine qua non* to experience authentic social bonds, since markets free people from vertical, asymmetric and unchosen relationships and create the conditions for a horizontal sociality between free and equal agents.

Thus within this tradition the market and the economic dimension are seen in *structural harmony with the social dimension*. An economic relationship is not different from a social relationship; rather, it is one form that expresses the dynamic of civil society: the market is civil society. Economic relationships are conceived as the new form of interpersonal relationship typical of commercial and large societies, distinct from, and in certain aspects opposed to, the typical relationships in communities, which are personal and based on strong bonds. In this formulation, the social sphere is coextensive with the economic sphere, which is distinct only from the private sphere (the family) and the political sphere (the state). From this perspective, developing markets means in and of itself developing civil society, which does not depend on gift or benevolence, but solely on contracts and conventions. In this vision – which is also an ideology – markets always and in all instances operate for the total good; they are the highest form of civil society, and any intervention at all, even for solidarity reasons (such as the Tobin Tax[1]), is seen as a hindrance, and thus harmful and immoral.

Opposing this first tradition we find authors who consider the economic and social realities in conflict with each other. This line of thought, which includes among its proponents such diverse authors as Marx, Polanyi, Weber and Simmel, considers the economic sphere to be sustained by principles that are substantially in conflict

---

1. A tax on all spot conversions of one currency into another in order to curb destabilizing movements of funds between foreign currencies proposed by the American macroeconomist (and Nobel Prize winner) James Tobin.

with those that sustain the social sphere. The market is conceived as an environment sustained by the principle of exchange, which is radically different from the principles that sustain both the political (the principle of authority) and the private and familial spheres (the principles of gift, gratuitousness, and so forth). And every time the market sphere escapes its orbit, tending to expand into adjacent spheres, it does so at the expense of the other two: the private sphere commercializes or politics becomes an instrumental exchange.

Thus it is not surprising that both these views strongly criticize the CSR movement. The first or so-called "liberal" vision, sees the company as *always* and by *nature* social, because by its actions in respecting laws and paying taxes it unintentionally produces the common good (wealth, development and work). From this perspective, any action that intentionally seeks to promote the social dimension will produce adverse effects for the company and society, because the company and its managers only have information to pursue the company's private good, and not the good of society. This is the ancient metaphor of the "invisible hand" used today although without Smith's philosophical refinement.

For the second vision, however, which is traditionally the more reform-minded, the capitalist company by its very nature *is never social*: its production relationships are based on unpaid work, theft and injustice, for which reasons the company destroys the social nexus. These authors also criticize the corporate social responsibility movement. In fact from this perspective, CSR is seen as deceptive, in that it presents a reality that is "ontologically" anti-social (as is the capitalist company) under the guise of pro-sociality, similar to whitewashing a tomb full of bones.

In reality, the discussion on CSR is more complex, requiring that one understand new cultural categories without excessive ideological conditioning. The first point to make is that when we talk about

CSR, we are dealing with a family of concepts and experiences, which we can attempt to group into three typologies:

1. Companies that adopt CSR practices only because they are constrained by civil or political pressure. These companies conceive of CSR as a cost to pay in order to operate, and if they change contexts (perhaps by moving elsewhere) those practices cease.

2. Companies that use CSR as a marketing and communication tool. Entrepreneurs know – either by instinct, market research, or because they operate in a sector with a high ethical impact – that consumers will reward them for associating social and ethical messages with their companies. In contrast with the first type, this second type freely chooses CSR, but not for intrinsic motives; if someday CSR is no longer advantageous, such practices will cease.

3. Companies that practice CSR for intrinsic motives, because entrepreneurs and those running the companies have internalized ethical values that lead them to act responsibly towards its various stakeholders and its territory. The CSR choice is not made primarily from a calculation of convenience, but from an internal and symbolic adherence to *identity codes*. For these reasons, there are as many forms of CSR practised by companies of the third type as there are experiences, given the close relationship between the way CSR is practised and the identity of the company itself. Just to cite a few examples: Olivetti (under Adriano Olivetti), the Banca Etica, the Economy of Communion, social cooperatives and cooperative credit unions, although all companies of the third type, represent experiences that differ widely among themselves. Each company shapes the CSR code, which takes the form of that particular organization, whereas type 1 and 2 companies adopt an external CSR ethical

code or protocol, and the company tries to model itself on that as best it can.

One might think that only the third type deserve the CSR name, and that we should be suspicious of the other two. This is not the case, however, because a market economy is civil *when it is able to combine all three forms of CSR.* What should be opposed are irresponsible companies that harm the social and natural environments; however, in this phase of capitalism, all three forms delineated are important for an economy and a society that want to grow in a balanced manner. Although outside the scope of this discussion, the third type, even if a minority, has the essential role of being the "starter" in settings with a low civil culture, and its presence determines the "civil quality" of economic development. But – and this is the crucial point – in a market made up only of irresponsible companies and type 3 companies, the latter inevitably would be destined for extinction; this outcome can only be avoided if type 1 and 2 companies *also* operate in the market.

The civilly responsible company

The increasingly widespread perception that the financial turbo-capitalist model may have exhausted its driving force offers a valuable occasion to rethink both the role of the company in this present historical phase and, more generally, the way we conceptualize the sense, the direction, of the market economy system. Socially responsible companies have certainly attained important goals on the frontline of civilizing the market. These are not enough. Even now, and increasingly in the near future, companies will be asked not only to produce wealth in a socially acceptable manner, but also to compete, along with the state and organized civil society, in redesigning the economic and institutional structures inherited from the recent past. In fact, it is no longer about settling for a company to respect the rules made by others – economic institutions are in substance nothing more than the rules of the economic game. Consider the rules for labour markets, banking systems, the structure of the fiscal system, the characteristics of the welfare model, and so forth. As agents and influential members of the market club, companies will be asked to contribute to rewriting the rules that have become obsolete or are incapable of guaranteeing the sustainability of integral human development.

In their 2012 work *Why Nations Fail*, Daron Acemoglu and James A. Robinson opportunely distinguished between extractive and inclusive economic institutions. The former favour transforming added value created by productive activity into parasitic rents, or they drive towards allocating resources into various forms of financial speculation. The latter, to the contrary, tend to facilitate including all resources (including labour) in the productive process, guaranteeing respect for basic human rights and the reduction of social inequalities. History persuasively points out that the decline – to the point of collapse – of a nation begins when extractive institutions predominate over inclusive institutions to the point of suffocating them.

A civilly responsible company is one that works with the forces available to it to accelerate the transition from an extractive institutional structure to an inclusive one. That means that it is no longer sufficient, as happens with the notion of social responsibility, for a company to aim to achieve *its own* objectives while satisfying the requirement to take into account the needs and identities of all classes of stakeholders. The notion of civil responsibility *further* requires that the goal itself of economic activity shift towards contributing to democratizing the market system. Where a socially responsible company aims to democratize its own internal governance, that is, to actualize so-called *democratic stakeholding*, the civilly responsible company *additionally* takes on the aim of competing with other actors to expand the degree of inclusivity in the market.

Phenomena of epochal import such as globalization and new technology revolutions tend to generate increasing levels of power asymmetry, jeopardizing the horizontal quality of intersubjective relationships between peers. In a time such as the present, in which the contract has become the principal tool for legal innovation as a new source of law and not merely an application of existing law, a civilly responsible company is one that understands that merely respecting contractual rules that do not derive from an authentic, deliberative democratic process does not insure the social and ethical sustainability of the market system. This is easy to grasp only if one considers that for more than a quarter of a century the market has been the primary place where power is exercised; consequently, it would be very difficult for politics alone to successfully check and give sensible direction to the economic process.

The events that accompanied the 2007–8 economic and financial crisis are the most eloquent confirmation of this genuinely new state of affairs. To give just one example, consider the "too big to fail" phenomenon. This effectively says that there are economic actors (e.g. banks and corporations) large and powerful enough to be capable of truly extorting national governments and which persist in moral hazard. This is why it is neither prudent nor wise to believe that the market is an ethically neutral space, or that a democratic polity is a force capable of keeping it in check and imparting a direction to it. If market actors themselves do not want inclusive rules of the game it will be difficult to guarantee a future social order in which liberty is not just liberty of choice, but above all the liberty to be able to choose (that is, the capability of choosing).

The centrality of the entrepreneur and of production

Today there is an extreme need, particularly in Italy, for entrepreneurs to rediscover social esteem, to again feel themselves to be constructing the common good, to stand apart from the many speculators and wheeler-dealers who have usurped the wonderful word "entrepreneur", to be the heirs of the medieval merchant and the pillars of every good and free society. We must truly and concretely give them a platform, let them speak, and listen to them. One of the major problems of every social theory is the absence of protagonists: we speak and write about labour, companies and workers, but there are no entrepreneurs, and they speak even in their absence.

In our many encounters during summer schools for young people, one of the most interesting experiences is the dialogue with those who have one or more entrepreneurial ideas. Every economics and management professor should have this sort of experience, particularly those of us who write books that seek to define the company and the role of the entrepreneur. The common element in the entrepreneurial ideas that flowed from these dialogues is a project to achieve, generally together with others. Profit is never mentioned; it remains in the background. This then is a first characteristic of the entrepreneur, of every entrepreneur who starts his own company: he wants to make a project happen, frequently linked to his own talents, dreams or opportunities. The project is the centre of the company.

However, when we hear a statement of this sort, "I want to make money during my lifetime and I am only looking to understand what activity is best adapted to meeting that goal" it is evident that we are dealing with very different actors. These individuals have no project around which to form a company; they have only a "project to make money", and they are looking for the most suitable company activity towards that end. Along with Luigi Einaudi and Giacomo Becattini, we call the first type "entrepreneurs" and the second type "speculators". Distinguishing these two types of economic actor does not mean attributing the first as "good" or the second as "bad": there are speculators who act entirely legally, create jobs, and at times offer good services to the community. It only means calling things by their correct names, recognizing that values such as gratuitousness, intrinsic motivations, vocation, positive passions and civil virtues are more likely to be found in the entrepreneur, the first type, and that wheeler-dealers more easily inhabit the second type.

In an economy different from ours, drawing this distinction between entrepreneurs and speculators would be sufficient to say many of the things we have written in this book – but not all. As defined here, entrepreneurs can include those who have plans to produce anti-personnel mines, pornography, or games of chance; these are projects as well, and there may be some few who pursue them, although against the common good (in reality these activities are carried out by speculators, and very frequently by wheeler-dealers with more or less organized criminal elements). This is why it is necessary within the family of entrepreneurs to distinguish the profile of the civil entrepreneur: an entrepreneur who pursues a project that she purposefully considers in the common good – that is, the good of each one and of all – and that is considered as such by the community and institutions in which she operates.

The profile of the civil entrepreneur may include artisans, co-operatives, social companies and companies in the Economy of Communion. But, it could also include public agencies created (as they should be) around a project for the common good. And where is the profit? There is profit, obviously, but that is not the primary reason for which the project was created. Profit is a signal or indicator that the project works, that it creates wealth and is sustainable. The civil entrepreneur does not have the goal of profit alone or of the maximization of profit, much less of positional rents. Thus while the speculator maximizes profit and ever increasing rents, in a civil company profit is one good element, but not its main purpose. It is one of the purposes, but not the only one, nor is it more important than the quality of the goods made, jobs created and preserved, faithfulness to the mission of the company, and so forth.

One decisive factor in this discourse is time. There is in fact a sort of "law" that, over time, entrepreneurs tend to become speculators. Frequently, although not always, large multinational corporations that originally formed around one project tend to become speculative over time. Since the ownership of their assets becomes spread across so many shareholders, managers are asked to maximize profits, possibly in the short term, by a myriad of anonymous owners (some of which are in turn made up of other myriads of anonymous actors, as in the case of large investment, pension or insurance funds). The speculator opens a shoe factory today, a construction firm tomorrow and a hospital the day after, all with the one purpose of making money *through* those activities.

An entrepreneur, as described by economists such as Joseph Schumpeter and Luigi Einaudi, is instead a different actor, because the primary scope of his activity is to realize a project, so much so that Becattini called such companies "project-companies". We repeat: profit is just one of many elements, serving primarily as an important and fundamental signal that the project is working, that it is innovative and growing over time. Thus an entrepreneur is someone who never completely "instrumentalizes" her company, because she attributes a certain intrinsic value to it; the company is an expression of an individual and collective life plan. That is true to the point that many entrepreneurs, particularly in these times, would make much more money closing their companies and investing the proceeds in speculative funds. They do not do so, however, because they see their companies as something more than a machine to make money: they see in it their identities and their life stories.

If we want to increase the quota of civility in our economies, we must tell different stories about capitalism, companies and life. For this we need artists, poets and writers, but we also need entrepreneurs who narrate stories with their lives, their creativity and their intelligence. By now it is well established that in the long run the competitive advantage of a nation depends on the civil fibre of its companies.

The responsibility of the citizen–consumer

We cannot leave the theme of civil responsibility, a theme we have developed to this point with reference to the company, without referring to the consumer, who also bears a non-trivial responsibility in contemporary society. Through to the end of the nineteenth century, consumption was seen as destruction. The work "consumption" itself in common speech was used to indicate the process of destruction. One consumed something to say that one was destroying it. Once consumed, it no longer exists. This is why frugality was the highest civic virtue of that period. Frugal behaviour was what deserved respect in the public sphere. Consumption belonged to the sphere of vices, so much so that when in 1713 Bernard Mandeville published his famous *The Fable of the Bees: or Private Vices, Publick Benefits*, his physical safety was at risk, having proposed an argument, too advanced for the spirit of his times, that consumption was a positive act while frugality – today we would say saving – is of negative value. Over two centuries passed before Keynes succeeded in again taking up and defending that theme.

Keynes made consumption the fundamental variable of his theory. His well-known *income multiplier* indicates that for an economy to develop, high levels of consumption must be maintained. Consumption as a destructive activity thus becomes a virtuous activity that keeps the overall mechanism in motion. These two concepts – consumption as destruction and consumption as a resource – are very different, but they have one element in common: they see consumption as a variable dependent on production. What directs the dance in the economic game is always production: in both the nineteenth- and twentieth-century versions, consumption was relegated to an ancillary role.

What is new in the current historical phase is the tendency to reverse the dependency relationship between consumption and production. Although fraught with many difficulties, consumption is becoming primary. John Stuart Mill's insight on "consumer sovereignty" in the second half of the nineteenth century (which was ahead of its time) is becoming true today. As Alfred Marshall (1842–1924), one of the founders of neoclassical economics, later stated on the same theme, consumers who choose between different companies are putting into practice the principle of substitution between offered goods, just as an entrepreneur chooses an optimal combination among production factors (Marshall 1920). The reality is that consumers have never been sovereign, nor are they today. However, consumers potentially have the ability to send messages to producers to persuade them to take into account the values that they, as consumers, believe in. By spending my money in one way rather than another I send a very precise signal to producers, not only communicating what I would like them to produce, but also the way I would like their products to be made. If consumers find out that sports shoes (referring to the famous Nike case) or some other product are made in a way they deem ethically unacceptable, they can sanction the producers economically through boycotts and public protests. This is the meaning of "voting with your wallet, or pocketbook", a notable example of social innovation.

The significant innovation of the present era is the emergence of the new figure of the *civilly responsible consumer*. Companies are not the only ones that must be civilly responsible; citizen–consumers cannot consider themselves exempt from the obligation to use their purchasing power to contribute towards attaining the goals they deem morally relevant. Consider that today about two-thirds of national income comes from private consumption expenditure. So it is easy to understand the significance of citizens' ethically oriented decisions on spending and saving. The same can be said about ethical finance, which is ethical in the sense that values are integral to agents' goals rather than functioning as external constraints; this is in addition to legal constraints, which in any case everyone must comply with. Note the difference. While in speculative finance ethical considerations constitute at best a reinforcement of one's own constraint system, in ethical finance they are a component of the objective function itself. This is the crux of the matter: responsible investors set achieving determined goals or respecting determined values as the purpose of their action constraints.

An example for us all. In 1971 Leon Sullivan, Baptist minister and civil rights leader, joined the General Motors board of directors in order to initiate a strategy of pressure on and disruption of the multinationals that contributed to sustaining the ignoble apartheid system in South Africa. His work was so successful that in 1977 he published the so-called Sullivan Principles, a set of seven principles that established a code of conduct for companies operating in South Africa and which became a sort of Magna Carta for activist shareholders. Until the mid-1990s the negative strategy of exclusion prevailed, in that investments were not made in sectors and/or companies whose actions were deemed reprehensible; beginning in

1995 a positive course of reward and engagement was followed, in that investments were used to direct or encourage specific actions by a company's management.

A significant recent result of the pressure exerted by the many civilly responsible consumer organizations was the approval in November 2011 of the Guiding Principles on Business and Human Rights by the United Nations Human Rights Council. The culmination of the 2008 adoption of the "Protect, Respect and Remedy" framework laid out by John Ruggie of Harvard University on behalf of the UN Secretary-General, these principles conclusively set forth companies' direct responsibility for respecting human rights in business activities, wherever they are located.

Another noteworthy example is that of the fair trade and solidarity movement, a virtuous economic practice started by the Dutch theologian Frans van der Hoff during the 1970s. Although the results of the fair trade movement are remarkable, that is not the only reason for which they should be carefully considered.[2] This example condenses one of the most important social innovations in the last quarter century. Having understood that it is possible to use the market and its logic to pursue freeing people from need and for strengthening fraternal bonds between them, this means recognizing that the core idea of the civil economy is actually practicable.

This is why the work of actors in the civil society is so crucial who, through their organizations, facilitate the exercise of virtuous behaviour by citizens. Persistent criticism by NGOs such as Oxfam, Global Justice Now, Food Watch and others in recent years has resulted in major banks (Deutsche Bank, Commerzbank and

---

2. The Dutch Max Havelaar foundation is present today in over twenty countries, and the Fairtrade Labelling Organization includes 162 organizations with over half a million producers of goods such as cacao and coffee.

DekaBank) and large pension funds (CalPERS and CalSTRS) ceasing to speculate on derivatives based on raw agricultural goods.[3]

We know that there are strong synergies between the phenomena of corporate social responsibility and discriminating consumption. It is completely normal that consumers' attention whose behaviour can be expressed by the slogan "consume better and be happier", rather than "consume more, pay less", is largely directed towards civil companies. At the same time, the expansion of civil companies broadens civil consumption.

As happened during the time of Civic Humanism, creating value today has once again come to require people, relationships and significance. Value is now produced by creating meaning through actions that create bonds, because they do not senselessly separate economic and social value. Civil companies and consumers have understood this; they recognize the existence of passions, ideals and human relationships that are not merchandise and cannot be treated as such. When this does happen – and it still happens frequently – corporate and individual good suffers negative consequences. Truly, if companies are just business – as bad teachers continue to teach – it is clear that they will succeed in attracting people of low relational quality, that is, managers and workers driven solely by extrinsic motivations. If the cultural signal that a company sends is exclusively based on profit, it is evident that such a signal will be picked up primarily by a certain type of people. But profit or power is too weak an incentive to stir people's higher energies, the most noble of which is liberty, which cannot be produced or bought. And where there is no liberty there cannot be creativity, much less the capacity to innovate.

---

3. The Forum for Sustainable and Responsible Investment estimated that in 2010 one dollar in eight invested in managed funds in the United States was in a socially responsible fund (see www.wssif.org/resources/sriguide/srifacts.cfm, accessed March 2016).

Epilogue

In closing this brief work, we want to call the reader's attention to a few foundational questions. Our intention is simply to suggest a way that the discourse initiated herein might continue. We have encountered people and ideas that, while differing among themselves, have made up the harmonious blend of notes and colours of this short book. As the Canadian economist and historian Jacob Viner liked to say, "Economics is what economists do" and the civil economy is what civil economists did and do, always keeping well in mind that the civil economy is not a school, or a research programme, much less an ideology. Rather, it is a paradigm, or a particular way of seeing reality.

We like to live out and think about the civil economy as a *process*, an inclusive and heterogeneous cultural movement, whose protagonists are not the adepts of a "church"; rather, they are people belonging to different historical periods, traditions and schools of thought, who are academics, entrepreneurs and young people, but who all hold a common understanding of the economy as civil engagement, pluralistic and attentive to life – not dogmatic, interdisciplinary and historical. Thus the writers and thinkers we have included in this book are neither the only, nor the most obvious, or classic (considered by an entire tradition as the foundational figures). Not all contemporary authors in the civil economy would agree in considering our selection as the founders of the civil economy, apart from Genovesi, and perhaps Dragonetti.

This pluralism of sources is a protection against an ideological and sectarian drift that every movement or cultural process faces. The cultural biodiversity of the civil economy is at once its strength and its weakness. On the one hand it enriches the civil economy; on the other it makes the process of defining strong identities for the actors involved slow and complex, it exposes it to abuse, and it requires working within a chaotic reality in constant movement – fortunately, a movement that is still in full development.

As we have outlined, one of the central themes of the civil economy tradition of thought is interpersonal relationships. Economists and social scientists do a disservice to themselves and to others if they continue to ignore intersubjectivity in explaining economic phenomena. It is truly paradoxical that mainstream economics has not noticed, at least to this point, the need to account for the natural sociability – which is very different to sociality – of the human person, given that economics since the dawn of the discipline has always been occupied with investigating the nature and dynamics of relationships between actors who live in society. Although the study of the relationship between people and the natural world is on the economist's agenda, this is not the signature trait of economic discourse – unless we want to reduce the discipline to a sort of social engineering.

The point in question is important and deserves emphasis. Classic culture taught us that there are three forms of reason: theoretical, practical and technical. Economics belongs, as seems obvious, to practical reason, but over the course of the centuries it has always maintained a privileged relationship with theoretical reason. Indeed, the great economists, whatever school of thought they belonged to, were also philosophers. Alfred Marshall noted that, yes, economics is the science of business, but it is also an essential part of the philosophical discourse on the human person. Or, as John Stuart Mill insisted, no one can be a good economist who is only an economist.

What is new in the last few decades is that economics has preferred to ally itself with technical reason, severing its ancient ties to theoretical reason. We see the consequences of that shift. Economic discourse has enormously increased its technical and analytical apparatus; however, it does not seem capable of grasping reality and is increasingly less capable of suggesting effective directions for action. We have in mind critical problems such as the endemic and accelerated increase in social inequality, the scandal of hunger, the eruption of conflicts over identity and their impact on the cause of peace, developmental sustainability, and the paradoxes of happiness. Although technique is necessary, it would be vain to think that these problems can be resolved with technical solutions. It is easy to grasp why. In epochal transitions, as is the current one, the technical reasoning of the natural sciences has little to offer economic discourse. They can suggest responses, but they cannot ask the right *questions*; economics today needs the right questions, above all the question of the human person.

The reductionist path taken by economic science over the last thirty years has ended up disarming critical thought, with the effects that are now evident to all. Believing that scientific rigour assumes a sterile neutrality, and that research, in order to be scientific, must free itself from all value references, has led to accepting libertarian individualism as a sort of pre-analytic assumption, one that requires no justification whatsoever, since it is considered a natural condition. We know however that this in and of itself is a very strong value judgement. Indeed, for individualism the individual is the only judge who attributes value to things and relationships in which one finds oneself. Since objective values do not exist, the individual is always the one who decides what is right or wrong, just or unjust, what is good and what is not.

But individualism alone would not be sufficient to account for the current state of "civilization and its discontents" (Freud [1930] 2010) if it were not tightly coupled with libertarianism, by those who think that grounding liberty and responsibility requires recourse to the idea of self-actualization. Only a self-actualized agent would be wholly free, or, as expressed by the British philosopher Galen Strawson (2004), one who is *causa sui*, which is impossible. Hence the idea derived from libertarian individualism – the real signature trait of the current individualistic revolution (the first was the Enlightenment) – that liberty assumes the dissolution of all bonds, and that every individual has the right to expand to the limits of his potential. In erroneously equating the notion of "bond" with "constraint", the conditionings of liberty (i.e. constraints) are confused with the conditions of liberty (i.e. bonds).

Reinterpreting the events of the recent economic and financial crisis through this conceptual lens allows us to go beyond the flood of tautological explanations so far produced. Michel Foucault was one thinker who, with rare perspicacity, understood this serious contradiction in second modernity. Confronting the problem of access to truth, he questioned whether we live in a time in which the market has become a "site of truth", a place where the entire lives of those involved are subsumed to economic efficiency, and where the market still ensures that for a government "to be a good government" it must operate according to this site of verediction:

> The market must tell the truth; it must tell the truth in rela-
> tion to government practice. Henceforth, and merely second-
> arily, it is its role of verediction that will command, dictate

and prescribe the jurisdictional mechanisms, or absence of such mechanisms, on which [the market] must be articulated.

(Foucault 2008: 32)

Actually, Foucault's and others' agitated preoccupation has profound roots. In his inaugural lecture for the new academic year at Oxford in October 1829, Richard Whately, the influential chair of political economy, stated for the first time the *non-overlapping magisteria* (NOMA) principle (see Emmett 2014). Whately's thesis was that if economics aspires to the status of a science it must separate itself from both ethics and politics. He divided the tasks as follows: ethics, the sphere of values, has the task of defining the norms that guide human behaviour; politics, the sphere of goals, has the task of democratically defining the objectives that society wants to attain; economics, the sphere of means, has the task of researching the most efficient ways to achieve those objectives with respect to those values. What need is there then for economics to maintain close ties with the other two spheres? For the economist, as a technician of means, the criterion of efficiency suffices as a guide for acting. Actually, Whately sought to mitigate the NOMA principle by speaking of distinctions between the spheres rather than separations, but with little success. Despite the objections of many non-influential voices, all successive economic thought more or less embraced this principle. Even today the majority of economics textbooks repeat with only minor variations the British economist, Lionel Robbins's famous definition: "Economics is the science which studies human behaviour as a relationship between given ends and scarce means which have alternative uses" (Robbins 1932: 16).

A development which is still difficult to grasp is that with the advent of globalization around the end of the 1970s, an unforeseen – but not unforeseeable – role reversal has been happening;

economics has become the sphere of ends, and politics has become the sphere of means. As many non-superficial observers have pointed out, contemporary democracy is at the service of the (uncivil) market. Limits of space allow us only to mention the one book: *The Map and the Territory* by Alan Greenspan (2013), president of the US Federal Reserve from 1987 to 2006, for an explicit confirmation by an authoritative witness. For about thirty years we have understood society as contained within the economy and democracy as a function of the market, instead of the contrary. The civil economy does not accept such a separation, for the obvious reason that the whole person is at the centre of its economic discourse. Autonomy, although doubtlessly necessary, cannot be pushed to the point of separation. We should never forget that the market is not just a mechanism for the efficient regulation of exchange. It is primarily an *ethos* that leads to profound changes in human relations and highlights people's character. This is why the civil economy insists that the principle of fraternity must be *within* the workings of the market, not outside, as "compassionate capitalism" claims.

Capitalism is one, but the varieties of capitalism are many, and the varieties depend on the cultural matrices prevalent in different historical epochs. Thus nothing in capitalism is irreversible. Civil economists certainly do not condemn wealth as such, and they certainly do not speak favourably about poverty. Quite the opposite. Rather, they want to discuss the *ways* in which wealth is created and the underlying *criteria* by which it is distributed among the members of human society, and the evaluation of these ways and criteria is certainly not of a technical nature. For example, civil economists do not accept the current version of social Darwinism that is effectively expressed in the Schumpeterian couplet "creative destruction", because this version reduces economic relationships between persons to relationships between things, and these things are ultimately merchandise. Above all they cannot accept *consensus facit iustum*, even if the expressed consensus is that of the majority.

From at least the time of Hobbes, a certain thought tradition has injudiciously taught that the social order can be established only with reference to two poles: the pole of force (that of violence, struggle and positional competition) and the pole of law (the social contract). However, consider the case of two perfect strangers: if they meet they cannot sign an agreement because they do not even have a common language to start negotiations. Thus, according to this thought tradition, they must necessarily fight. Or not. One of them may decide to make a gift and discover that the social order can follow from that, as history teaches us. The latter course is preferred by those located in the civil economy stream, which is against both gifts without exchange and exchange without gifts, or pure commercial exchange between strangers. In the long run, exchange without reciprocity destroys the market. Visible reciprocity constitutes the theoretical counterpart to the invisible hand of exchange.

The philosopher John L. Austin wrote about the "performativity" of a scientific paradigm to signify the transformative influence of that paradigm on reality. It is true that paradigms, along with other scientific theories, do not just suggest lines of action; they change people's mindset. Today we are becoming more and more aware that a computational mindset, however much it might grip the intellect, is insufficient – though still necessary – to remedy the expanding cultural poverty of economic discourse. The intellect can in fact calculate, but only the humanity of the person can produce engaged thought. This is the great challenge of today, a challenge that the civil economy intends to take up and possibly win.

References

Acemoglu, D. & J. A. Robinson 2012. *Why Nations Fail: The Origins of Power, Prosperity and Poverty*. New York: Crown.

Arendt, H. [1958] 1998. *The Human Condition*. Chicago, IL: University of Chicago Press.

Aristotle. *Politics*, B. Jowett (trans.), http://classics.mit.edu/Aristotle/politics.html (accessed 10 June 2016).

Beccaria, C. [1764] 1995. *Dei delitti e delle pene* [*On Crimes and Punishments*]. In *On Crimes and Punishments and Other Writings*, R. Bellamy (ed.), R. Davies (trans.). Cambridge: Cambridge University Press.

Benedict, R. 2005. *The Chrysanthemum and the Sword*. Boston, MA: Houghton Mifflin.

Bianchini, L. 1855. *Della scienza del bene vivere sociale* [*On the Science of Social Well-Living*]. Naples: Reale.

Bruni, L. 2012. *The Wound and the Blessing: Economics, Relationships, and Happiness*. Hyde Park, NY: New City Press.

Bruni, L. & S. Zamagni 2007. *Civil Economy*. Oxford: Peter Lang.

Bruni, L. & S. Zamagni 2014. "Economics and Theology in Italy Since the Eighteenth Century". In *The Oxford Handbook of Christianity and Economics*, P. Oslington (ed.), 57–72. Oxford: Oxford University Press.

Chiapello, E. & L. Boltansky 2007. *The New Spirit of Capitalism*, G. Elliot (trans.). London: Verso.

Coman, K. 1911. "Some Unsettled Problems of Irrigation". *American Economic Review* **1**(5): 1–19.

Doria, P. M. 1852. *Della vita civile* [*Civil Life*]. Turin: Cugini Pomba.

Dragonetti, G. 1766. *Delle virtù e de' premi* [*On Virtues and Rewards*]. Genoa: Gravier.

Dragonetti, G. 1788. *Sull'origine dei feudi* [*On the Origins of Fiefs*]. Milan: Regale.

Dudley, W. 2014. "Enhancing Financial Stability by Improving Culture in the Financial Services Industry". Workshop on Reforming Culture and Behavior in the Financial Services Industry, Federal Reserve Bank of New York, New York, 20 October, www.newyorkfed.org/newsevents/speeches/2014/dud141020a.html (accessed December 2015).

Emmett, R. B. 2014. "Economics and Theology after Separation". In *The Oxford Handbook of Christianity and Economics*, P. Oslington, (ed.), 135–50. Oxford: Oxford University Press.

Fanfani, A. 1942. *Il volontarismo* [*Voluntarism*]. Como: Cavalleri.

Fanfani, A. 1968. *Storia economica, I: Antichità, Medioevo, età moderna* [*Economic History, I: Antiquity, the Middle Ages, and the Modern Age*]. Turin: UTET.

Fanfani, A. [1976] 2002. *Capitalism, Collectivity and Participation*. Norfolk, VA: IHS Press.

Fanfani, A. [1991] 2014. *Tre rivoluzioni industriali, due guerre mondiali, ed ora?* [*Three Industrial Revolutions, Two World Wars, and Now?*]. In *Dall'Eden alla Terza guerra mondiale* [*From Eden to the Third World War*], M. Poettinger (ed.). Florence: Polistampa.

Ferrara, F. 1850. *Biblioteca dell'economista* [*Economist's Library*]. Torino: Cugini Pomba.

Filangieri, G. [1780] 2003. *La scienza della legislazione* [*The Science of Legislation*], V. Ferrone (ed.). Critical edition. Venice: Centro di Studi sull'Illuminismo Europeo "G. Stiffoni".

Foucault, M. 2008. *The Birth of Biopolitics*. Basingstoke: Palgrave Macmillan.

Freud, S. [1930] 2010. *Civilization and Its Discontents*. New York: W. W. Norton.

Frischmann, B. M. 2012. *Infrastructure: The Social Value of Shared Resources*. Oxford: Oxford University Press.

Fuà, G. 1993. *Crescita economica: L'insidia delle cifre* [*Economic Growth: The Snare in the Numbers*]. Bologna: Il Mulino.

Galiani, F. [1751] 1780. *Della Moneta* [*On Money*]. Naples: Simoniana.

Gauthier, D. 1986. *Morals by Agreement*. Oxford: Clarendon Press.

Genovesi, A. 1754. *Discorso sopra il vero fine delle lettere e delle scienze* [*Discourse on the True Purpose of the Letters and Sciences*]. Naples: [publisher not identified].

Genovesi, A. [1757] 2005. *Elementi di commercio* [*Elements of Commerce*]. In *Lezioni di commercio o sia di economia civile* [*Lessons of Commerce or Civil Economy*], M. L. Perna (ed.), critical edition. Naples: Istituto Italiano per gli Studi Filosofici.

Genovesi, A. 1758. *Meditazioni filosofiche sulla religione, e sulla morale* [*Philosophical Meditations on Religion and Morality*]. Naples: Simoniana.

Genovesi, A. 1765–70. *Lezioni di economia civile* [*Lessons of Civil Economy*]. Naples: Cugini Pomba.

Genovesi, A. 1766a. *Diceosina o sia della filosofia del giusto e dell'onesto* [*Diceosina, or the Philosophy of the Just and the Honest*]. Naples: Simoniana.

Genovesi, A. 1766b. *Logica* [*Logic*]. Naples: Simoniana.

Genovesi, A. [1769] 2005. *Lezioni di commercio o sia di economia civile* [*Lessons of Commerce or Civil Economy*], M. L. Perna (ed.), critical edition. Naples: Istituto Italiano per gli Studi Filosofici.

Genovesi, A. 1963. *Autobiografia, lettere e altri scritti* [*Autobiography, Letters and Other Writings*]. Milan: Feltrinelli.

Gioia, M. 1818. *Del merito e delle ricompense: Trattato storico e filosofico* [*On Merit and Recompense: a Historical and Philosophical Treatise*]. Milan: Gio. Pirotta.

Greenspan, A. 2013. *The Map and the Territory: Risk, Human Nature, and the Future of Forecasting*. London: Penguin.

Gregory, B. S. 2012. *The Unintended Reformation: How a Religious Revolution Secularized Society*. Cambridge, MA: Harvard University Press.

Gregory, T. 2013. *Principe di questo mondo* [*Prince of This World*]. Rome: Laterza.

Hardin, G. 1968. "The Tragedy of the Commons". *Science* **162**(3859) (December): 1243–8.

Hayek, F. [1937] 1996. "Economics and Knowledge". In his *Individualism and Economic Order*, 33–56. Chicago, IL: University of Chicago Press.

Hevesi, D. 2008. "Michael Hammer, Business Writer, Dies at 60". *New York Times* (5 September), www.nytimes.com/2008/09/05/business/05hammer.html (accessed 11 June 2016).

Hobbes, T. 1676. *Leviathan, or The Matter, Forme and Power of a Common Wealth Ecclesiasticall and Civil*. London: Andrew Crooke.

Keynes, J. M. 1939. "Democracy and Efficiency". *New Statesman and Nation* (28 January): 121–3.

Labriola, A. 1912. *Il valore della scienza economica* [*The Value of Economic Science*]. Naples: Società Editrice Partenopea.

Latouche, S. 2000. *La sfida di Minerva* [*Minerva's Challenge*]. Turin: Bollati Boringhieri. First published in French.

Laveleye, É. de 1874. *De la propriété et de ses formes primitive* [*On Property and Its Primitive Forms*]. Paris: Librairie G. Baillière.

Leopardi, G. [1824] 1906. *Discorso sopra lo stato presente dei costumi degli italiani* [*Discourse on the Present State of the Manners of the Italians*]. In G. Leopardi,

Scritti Inediti dalle carte napoletane [*Unpublished Works from the Neapolitan Papers*]. Florence: Successori Le Monnier.

Liddell, H. G. & R. Scott 1968. *A Greek–English Lexicon*. Oxford: Clarendon Press.

Loria, A. 1880. *La rendita fondiaria e la sua elisione naturale* [*Land Rent and its Natural Elision*]. Milan: Ulrico Hoepli.

Loria, A. 1889. *Analisi della proprietà capitalista* [*An Analysis of Capitalist Property*]. Turin: Bocca.

Loria, A. 1899. *La costituzione economica* [*The Economic Constitution*]. Turin: Bocca.

Loria, A. 1901. *Il capitalismo e la scienza* [*Capitalism and Science*]. Turin: Bocca.

Loria, A. 1902. *Le basi economiche della costituzione sociale* [*The Economic Bases of the Constitution of Society*]. Turin: Bocca.

Loria, A. 1904. *Verso la giustizia sociale* [*Towards Social Justice*]. Milan: Società Editrice Libraria.

Loria, A. 1909. *La sintesi economica* [*An Economic Summary*]. Turin: Bocca.

Loria, A. 1910. *Corso completo di economia politica* [*A Complete Course in Political Economy*]. Milan: Bocca.

Loria, A. 1947. *Una crociera eccezionale* [*An Exceptional Journey*]. Milan: Bocca.

Luther, M. [1520] 1915. *An Open Letter to the Christian Nobility of the German Nation, Concerning the Reform of the Christian Estate*, C. M. Jacobs (trans.). Philadelphia, PA: Lutheran Publication Society.

Madison, J., A. Hamilton & J. Jay 1788. *The Federalist; or, The New Constitution*, 2 vols. New York: J. and A. McLean.

Mandeville, B. [1713] 1988. *The Fable of the Bees: or Private Vices, Publick Benefits*. Indianapolis, IN: Liberty Fund.

Margalit, A. 1996. *The Decent Society*. Cambridge, MA: Harvard University Press.

Maritain, J. [1936] 1974. *Integral Humanism*. Notre Dame, IN: University of Notre Dame Press.

Marshall, A. 1920. *Principles of Economics*. London: Macmillan and Co.

Marx, K. [1894] 1909. *Capital*, vol. III. Chicago, IL: Charles H. Kerr.

Muratori, L. A. 1749. *Della pubblica felicità, oggetto de' buoni principi* [*On Public Happiness, the Goal of Good Principles*]. Lucca: [publisher not identified].

Nussbaum, M. 1986. *The Fragility of Goodness*. Cambridge: Cambridge University Press.

Olivetti, A. [1955] 2012. *Ai lavoratori* [*To the Workers*]. Rome: Edizioni di Communità.

Ostrom, E. 1990. *Governing the Commons*. Cambridge: Cambridge University Press.

Pantaleoni, M. 1889. *Principi di economia pura* [*Principles of Pure Economics*]. Florence: Barbera.

Pantaleoni, M. 1925. *Erotemi di economia [Economic Questions]*, vol. 1. Bari: Laterza.

Perroux, F. 1962. *Le capitalisme*. Paris: Presses universitaires de France.

Piketty, T. 2014. *Capital in the Twenty-First Century*. Cambridge, MA: Harvard University Press.

Rawls, J. 1971. *A Theory of Justice*. Cambridge, MA: Harvard University Press.

Robbins, L. 1932. *An Essay on the Nature and Significance of Economic Science*. London: Macmillan.

Ruskin, J. [1860] 1901. *Unto This Last*. New York: Thomas Y. Crowell.

Shiller, R. 2012. *Finance and the Good Society*. Princeton, NJ: Princeton University Press.

Smith, A. [1759] 1982. *The Theory of Moral Sentiments*. Indianapolis, IN: Liberty Fund.

Smith, A. [1776] 1981. *An Inquiry into the Nature and Causes of the Wealth of Nations*. Indianapolis, IN: Liberty Fund.

Sorrentino, D. 2012. *Giuseppe Toniolo: l'economista di Dio [Giuseppe Toniolo: God's Economist]*. Rome: AVE.

Strawson, G. 2004. "Free Agents". *Philosophical Topics* **32**(2): 371–402.

Taylor, F. 1911. *The Principles of Scientific Management*. New York: Harper & Brothers.

Tocqueville, A. de. 2010. *Democracy in America*. Indianapolis, IN: Liberty Fund.

Verri, P. [1763] 1963. *Meditazioni sulla felicità [Meditations on Happiness]*. Milan: Feltrinelli.

Weber, M. 2008. *The Protestant Ethic and the Spirit of Capitalism*. Chicago, IL: BN Publishing.

Williams, B. 1993. *Shame and Necessity*. Berkeley, CA: University of California Press.

Zamagni, S. 2010. "Catholic Social Thought, Civil Economy and the Spirit of Capitalism". In *The True Wealth of Nations*, D. Finn (ed.), 63–94. Oxford: Oxford University Press.

Zamagni, S. 2015. "Beni Comuni e Economia Civile" ["Common Goods and Civil Economy"]. In *Beni Comuni e Cooperazione*, L. Sacconi & S. Ottone (eds). Bologna: Il Mulino.

Further reading

Benjamin, W. [1921] 2005. "Capitalism as Religion [Fragment 74]", C. Kautzer (trans.). In *Religion as Critique: The Frankfurt School's Critique of Religion*, E. Mendieta (ed.), 259–62. Abingdon: Routledge.

Bruni, L. 2006. *Civil Happiness*. Abingdon: Routledge.

Bruni, L. 2012b. *The Genesis of the Ethos of the Market*. Basingstoke: Palgrave Macmillan.

D'Onofrio, F. 2015. "On the Concept of 'Felicitas Publica' in Eighteenth Century Political Economy". *Journal of the History of Economic Thought* **37** (September): 449–71.

Frey, B. 1997. *Not Just for the Money*. Cheltenham: Edward Elgar.

Grant, R. W. 2012. *Strings Attached: Untangling the Ethics of Incentives*. Princeton, NJ: Princeton University Press.

Hirschman, A. O. 1977. *The Passions and the Interests: Political Arguments for Capitalism before its Triumph*. Princeton, NJ: Princeton University Press.

MacIntyre, A. 1981. *After Virtue*. Notre Dame, IN: University of Notre Dame Press.

Mauss, M. [1922] 1990. *The Gift: Forms and Functions of Exchange in Archaic Societies*. London: Routledge.

Milankovic, B. 2011. *The Haves and the Have-Nots*. New York: Basic Books.

Milbank, J. 2006. *Theology and Social Theory: Beyond Secular Reason*. Oxford: Wiley-Blackwell.

Kosfeld, M. & S. Neckermann 2011. "Getting More Work for Nothing? Symbolic Awards and Worker Performance". *American Economic Journal: Microeconomics* (3 August): 86–99.

Pabst, A. 2011. "From Civil to Political Economy: Adam Smith's Theological Debt". In *Adam Smith as Theologian*, P. Oslington (ed.), 106–24. Abingdon: Routledge.

Paine, T. [1776] 2016. *Common Sense*. Los Angeles, CA: Enhanced Media Publishing.

Polanyi, K. [1944] 2001. *The Great Transformation: The Political and Economic Origins of Our Time*. Boston, MA: Beacon Press.

Reinert, S. 2010. "Lessons on the Rise and Fall of Great Powers: Conquest, Commerce, and Decline in Enlightenment Italy". *American Historical Review* **115**(5): 1395–425.

Robertson, J. 2005. *The Case for the Enlightenment: Scotland and Naples, 1680–1760*. Cambridge: Cambridge University Press.

Sandel, M. 2010. *Justice: What's the Right Thing to Do?* London: Penguin.

Screpanti, E. & S. Zamagni 2005. *An Outline of the History of Economic Thought*. Oxford: Oxford University Press.

Sen, A. 2010. *The Idea of Justice*. London: Allen Lane.

Venturi, F. 1972. *Italy and the Enlightenment*. London: Longman.

Wootton, D. 1994. *Republicanism, Liberty, and Commercial Society, 1649–1776*. Palo Alto, CA: Stanford University Press.

Index